COMMON CORE

LANGUAGE ARTS
&
LITERACY

Activities that Captivate, Motivate, & Reinforce

REVISED EDITION

Grade 2

by Marjorie Frank

IncentivePublications

BY WORLD BOOK

Illustrated by Kathleen Bullock
Cover by Penny Laporte

Print Edition ISBN 978-0-86530-738-4
E-book Edition ISBN 978-1-62950-196-3 (PDF)

World Book, Inc.
180 North LaSalle Street
Suite 900
Chicago, Illinois 60601
U.S.A.

For information about World Book and Incentive Publications products, call **1-800-967-5325,** or visit our websites at **www.worldbook.com** and **www.incentivepublications.com.**

Printed in the United States of America by Mercury Print Productions, Rochester, New York

CONTENTS

Introduction

Great Support for Common Core State Standards! 7

How to Use This Book 7

About Common Core State Standards for Language Arts & Literacy 8

Grade 2 Common Core State Standards for Language Arts & Literacy

College and Career Readiness Anchor Standards for Reading, Grades K-12 9

Reading Standards for Literature, Grade 2 10

Reading Standards for Informational Text, Grade 2 11

Reading Standards: Foundational Skills for Grade 2 12

College and Career Readiness Anchor Standards for Writing, Grades K-12 13

Writing Standards, Grade 2 14

College and Career Readiness Anchor Standards
for Speaking and Listening, Grades K-12 15

Speaking and Listening Standards, Grade 2 16

College and Career Readiness Anchor Standards for Language, Grades K-12 . . . 17

Language Standards, Grade 2 18

Reading—Literature

Being Lost Is No Fun (key ideas, details) 22

School in a Tree (key ideas, details) 23

A Deep-Sea Scare (key ideas, details) 24

Silly Sentences (key ideas, details) 25

The Lion and the Mouse (key ideas, details, characters) 26

The Tale of the Elephant's Nose (key ideas, details, characters) 27

The Big Game (key ideas, details, characters) 28

The Shopping Trip (key ideas, details, characters) 29

Classroom Rules (words, rhythm, meaning) 30

School Supplies (words, rhythm, meaning) 31

The Great Hit (story structure) 32

Math Mix-Up *(text structure)* 33

Cloud Watching *(point of view, characters)* 34

A Picnic Memory *(information from illustrations)* 35

Dressed for Drama *(information from illustrations)* 36

Talent Show *(information from illustrations)* 37

Lost Name Tags *(information from illustrations)* 38

Playground Fun *(compare, contrast)* 39

Reading—Informational Text

Picnic Tummy Aches *(key ideas, details)* 42

A Report on Gilas *(key ideas, details)* 43

Detective's Helper *(key ideas, details)* 44

To Market, to Market! *(key ideas, details)* 45

Body Parts You Can't See *(key ideas, details)* 46

Something's Missing *(connections to content-area topics)* 47

Which Happened First? *(connections to content-area topics)* 48

Who Can You Call? *(academic vocabulary)* 49

How Those Animals Behave! *(academic vocabulary)* 50

Picture Stories to Finish *(text features)* 51

What Do Bees Know? *(author's purpose)* 52

Job Search *(author's purpose)* 53

Follow the Parade! *(information from illustrations)* 54

Circus, Circus *(information from illustrations)* 55

Who Gets the Milk? *(information from illustrations)* 56

Rafting on the River *(supporting reasons)* 57

Benjy's List *(supporting reasons)* 58

Disappearing Dinosaurs *(compare, contrast)* 59

Reading—Foundational Skills

An A-B-C Adventure *(phonics, word recognition, vowel sounds)* 62

Clowning Around *(phonics, word recognition, vowel sounds)* 63

Moose Tracking *(phonics, word recognition, vowel sounds)* 64

Rhino Watching *(phonics, word recognition, vowel sounds)* 65

A Helicopter Flight *(phonics, word recognition, vowel sounds)*..............66

Hurricane Watch *(phonics, word recognition, vowel sounds)*..............67

Reptile Races *(phonics, word recognition, vowel sounds)*..............68

Visit a Desert Hotel *(phonics, word recognition, prefixes, suffixes)*..............69

Nighttime Detectives *(phonics, prefixes, suffixes, roots)*..............70

Rodeo Ride *(phonics, prefixes, suffixes, roots)*..............71

Ski the Alps *(phonics, spelling-sound correspondence)*..............72

Through the Iceberg Maze *(phonics, spelling-sound correspondence)*..............73

A Thrilling Ride *(phonics, spelling-sound correspondence)*..............74

What's That Under the Sea? *(word recognition, irregularly spelled words)*..............75

The Wild Boar Chase *(word recognition, irregularly spelled words)*..............76

Deep in the Rain Forest *(word recognition, irregularly spelled words)*..............77

A Twirling Ride *(word recognition, irregularly spelled words)*..............78

Writing

Choose Your Adventure *(text types: opinion)*..............80

A Swamp Cruise *(text types: opinion)*..............82

Over the Edge *(text types: opinion)*..............83

Meet the Meat Eaters *(text types: informative/explanatory)*..............84

Hunt for Pirate Treasure *(text types: informative/explanatory)*..............85

Fire Danger! *(text types: informative/explanatory)*..............86

Search for Bigfoot *(text type: narrative)*..............87

Underwater Surprises *(text type: narrative)*..............88

Go Spelunking! *(develop and revise writing)*..............89

A Bumpy Camel Ride *(develop and revise writing)*..............90

A Low-Down Place *(develop and revise writing)*..............91

A Lot of Hot Air *(develop and revise writing)*..............92

Time Travel *(recall and write from experience)*..............93

Alaska Campout *(recall and write from experience)*..............94

Language

Milton the Magnificent *(conventions: nouns, collective nouns)*..............96

Step Right Up! *(conventions: plural nouns)*..............97

Monkey Action (*conventions: past tense verbs*) 98

Take a Spin (*conventions: reflexive pronouns*) 100

The Champion (*conventions: adjectives and adverbs*) 101

Adventures on the High Wire (*conventions: adverbs*) 102

Leaping Through Fire (*conventions: sentences*) 103

A Bunch of Balloons (*conventions: sentences*) 104

Unusual Talents (*conventions: sentences*) 105

Ups and Downs (*conventions: capitalization*) 106

Letters from the Circus (*conventions: punctuation—commas*) 107

On the Merry-Go-Round (*conventions: punctuation—apostrophes*) 108

Weird, Wacky Mirrors (*conventions: spelling*) 109

Sniffing Out Mistakes (*conventions: spelling*) 110

Fun on the Circus Train (*conventions: spelling*) 111

Ring-Toss Talk (*knowledge of language: language use*) 112

Mystery on the Train (*vocabulary: word meaning, context*) 113

The Great Taco Mystery (*vocabulary: word meaning, context*) 114

Safety on the Slopes (*vocabulary: word meaning, prefixes*) 115

Track the Mountain Gorilla (*vocabulary: word meaning, suffixes*) 116

Twice as Nice (*vocabulary: multiple meanings*) 117

Double the Fun (*vocabulary: word meaning, roots*) 118

Two Words Make New Words (*vocabulary: word meaning, compounds*) 119

What Would You Do With It? (*vocabulary: word meaning, dictionary use*) 120

Catch a Great Wave (*vocabulary: word relationships*) 121

A Stop at the Pastry Shop (*vocabulary: word relationships*) 122

Word Relatives (*vocabulary: shades of meaning*) 123

Carnival Words (*acquired vocabulary*) 124

Look Again! (*vocabulary: shades of meaning*) 126

Assessment and Answer Keys

Language Arts & Literacy Assessment 128

Assessment Answer Key 139

Activities Answer Key 140

Great Support for
Common Core State Standards!

Invite your students to join in on mysteries and adventures with colorful characters! They will delight in the high-appeal topics and engaging visuals. They can

> . . . track down Bigfoot and a goofy moose,
>
> . . . convince someone to wrestle an alligator,
>
> . . . join some monkeys in a barrel of fun,
>
> . . . chase a wild boar through a word puzzle,
>
> . . . wander through a Hall of Wacky Mirrors,
>
> . . . solve a mystery on a train at midnight,
>
> . . . teach a knight how to tame a fire-breathing dragon,
>
> . . . navigate through a maze of icebergs,
>
> . . . and tackle many other engaging escapades.

And while they enjoy these adventures, they will be moving toward competence in critical language skills and standards that they need for success in the real world.

How to Use This Book

- The pages are tools to support your teaching of the concepts, processes, and skills outlined in the Common Core State Standards. This is not a curriculum; it is a collection of engaging experiences for you to use as you work with your students or children.

- Use any given page to introduce, explain, teach, practice, extend, assess, start a discussion about, or get students collaborating on a skill or concept.

- Use any page in a large-group or small-group setting to deepen understandings and expand knowledge or skills. **Pages are not meant to be used as independent work. Guide students in their use. Do them together. Review and discuss the work with students.**

- Each activity is focused on a particular standard or cluster of standards, but most make use of or can be expanded to strengthen other standards as well.

- The book is organized according to the Common Core language strands. Use the tables on pages 9 to 19, the page labels, and notations on the Contents pages to identify the standards supported by each page.

- Use the suggestions on page 8 for further mastery of the Common Core State Standards for Language Arts & Literacy.

About Common Core State Standards for Language Arts & Literacy

The Common Core State Standards for Language Arts & Literacy at Grade 2 aim to build strong content knowledge across a wide range of subject areas. They are also designed to develop capabilities for thoughtful use of technology and digital media; for finding, applying, and evaluating evidence; for working and thinking independently; and for deep reasoning and understanding. To best help students gain and master these robust standards for reading, writing, speaking, listening, and language:

1. Know the standards well. Keep them in front of you. Understand for yourself the big picture of what the standards seek to do. (See www.corestandards.org.)

2. Work to apply, expand, and deepen student skills. With activities in this book (or any learning activities), plan to include

    . . . interaction with peers in pairs, small groups, and large groups.

    . . . plenty of discussion and integration of language content.

    . . . emphasis on asking questions, analyzing, careful reading, listening, finding evidence, and reasoning.

    . . . lots of observation, meaningful feedback, follow-up, and reflection.

3. Ask questions that advance reasoning, discernment, relevance, and real-life connection:

   - *Why? What does this mean?*
   - *How do you know?*
   - *What led you to this conclusion?*
   - *Where did you find this?*
   - *What else do you know (or need to know)?*
   - *What is the evidence?*
   - *Where else could you look?*
   - *How is ____ like (or unlike) ____?*
   - *What would be another viewpoint?*
   - *Why do you think that?*
   - *What is the purpose?*
   - *What belief does the author have?*
   - *Do you agree? Why or why not?*
   - *How are the words used?*
   - *What are the parts? How do they work together?*

   - *How does this part affect that part?*
   - *Where have you seen something like this before?*
   - *How does this affect your life?*
   - *How would this differ for a different purpose (or place, person, or situation)?*
   - *How does the idea of the text (or speech or argument) build?*
   - *How is this idea affected by the ideas that came before it?*
   - *How could you write (or say) this to give ____ effect?*
   - *What is the effect of using this word (or phrase, or idea, or structure)?*
   - *How is this affected by the writer's (or speaker's) perspective or culture?*
   - *So what? (What difference does this information, perspective, or discovery make?)*

8

Grade 2 Common Core State Standards
for Language Arts & Literacy

College and Career Readiness Anchor Standards (CCRS) for Reading, Grades K–12

Standard Number	Standard	Pages that Support
Key Ideas and Details		
CCRA.R.1	Read closely to determine what the text says explicitly and to make logical inferences from it; cite specific textual evidence when writing or speaking to support conclusions drawn from the text.	22, 23, 24, 25, 26, 27, 28, 29, 30, 31, 32, 33, 34, 35, 36, 37, 38, 39-40, 42, 43, 44, 45, 46, 47, 48, 49, 50, 51, 52, 53, 54, 55, 56, 57, 58, 59-60
CCRA.R.2	Determine central ideas or themes of a text and analyze their development; summarize the key supporting details and ideas.	21, 22, 23, 24, 25, 26, 27, 28, 29, 46, 52, 53
CCRA.R.3	Analyze how and why individuals, events, and ideas develop and interact over the course of a text.	22, 25, 26, 27, 28, 29, 47, 48, 49, 50, 51
Craft and Structure		
CCRA.R.4	Interpret words and phrases as they are used in a text, including determining technical, connotative, and figurative meanings, and analyze how specific word choices shape meaning or tone.	30, 31, 50, 52, 53,
CCRA.R.5	Analyze the structure of texts, including how specific sentences, paragraphs, and larger portions of the text (e.g., a section, chapter, scene, or stanza) relate to each other and the whole.	32, 33, 34, 42, 50, 51, 52, 57
CCRA.R.6	Assess how point of view or purpose shapes the content and style of a text.	33, 34, 52, 53
Integration of Knowledge and Ideas		
CCRA.R.7	Integrate and evaluate content presented in diverse media and formats, including visually and quantitatively, as well as in words.	39-40
CCRA.R.8	Delineate and evaluate the argument and specific claims in a text, including the validity of the reasoning as well as the relevance and sufficiency of the evidence.	22, 28, 29, 31, 34, 35, 57, 58
CCRA.R.9	Analyze how two or more texts address similar themes or topics in order to build knowledge or to compare the approaches the authors take.	39-40, 59-60
Range of Reading and Level of Text Complexity		
CCRA.R.10	Read and comprehend complex literary and informational texts independently and proficiently.	22-40, 42-60

Common Core Reinforcement Activities: 2nd Grade Language

Reading Standards for Literature, Grade 2

Standard Number	Standard	Pages that Support
Key Ideas and Details		
RL.2.1	Ask and answer such questions as *who, what, where, when, why,* and *how* to demonstrate understanding of key details in a text.	22, 23, 24, 25, 26, 27, 28, 29, 30, 31, 32, 33, 34, 35, 36, 37, 38, 39-40
RL.2.2	Recount stories, including fables and folktales from diverse cultures; determine the central message, lesson, or moral.	26, 27
RL.2.3	Describe how characters in a story respond to major events and challenges.	22, 25, 26, 27, 28, 29
Craft and Structure		
RL.2.4	Describe how words and phrases (e.g., regular beats, alliteration, rhymes, repeated lines) supply rhythm and meaning in a story, poem, or song.	30, 31
RL.2.5	Describe the overall structure of a story, including describing how the beginning introduces the story and the ending concludes the action.	32, 33, 34
RL.2.6	Acknowledge differences in the points of view of characters, including by speaking in a different voice for each character when reading dialogue aloud.	33, 34
Integration of Knowledge		
RL.2.7	Use information gained from the illustrations and words in a print or digital text to demonstrate understanding of its characters, setting, or plot.	23, 24, 31, 35, 36, 37, 38, 39-40
RL.2.8	(not applicable to literature)	
RL.2.9	Compare and contrast two or more versions of the same story (e.g., Cinderella stories) by different authors or from different cultures.	39-40
Range of Reading and Level of Text Complexity		
RL.2.10	By the end of the year, read and comprehend literature, including stories, and poetry, in the grades 2–3 text complexity band proficiently, with scaffolding as needed at the high end of the range.	22-40

Reading Standards for Informational Text, Grade 2

Standard Number	Standard	Pages that Support
Key Ideas and Details		
RI.2.1	Ask and answer such questions as *who, what, where, when, why,* and *how* to demonstrate understanding of key details in a text.	42, 43, 44, 45, 46, 47, 48, 49, 50, 52, 53, 57, 58, 59-60
RI.2.2	Identify the main topic of a multiparagraph text as well as the focus of specific paragraphs within the text.	46, 52, 53
RI.2.3	Describe the connection between a series of historical events, scientific ideas or concepts, or steps in technical procedures in a text.	47, 48, 49, 50, 51
Craft and Structure		
RI.2.4	Determine the meaning of words and phrases in a text relevant to a grade 2 topic or subject area.	50, 52, 53
RI.2.5	Know and use various text features (e.g., captions, bold print, subheadings, glossaries, indexes, electronic menus, icons) to locate key facts or information in a text efficiently.	42, 50, 51, 52, 57
RI.2.6	Identify the main purpose of a text, including what the author wants to answer, explain, or describe.	52, 53
Integration of Knowledge		
RI.2.7	Explain how specific images (e.g., a diagram showing how a machine works) contribute to and clarify a text.	42, 43, 44, 45, 46
RI.2.8	Describe how reasons support specific points the author makes in a text.	57, 58
RI.2.9	Compare and contrast the most important points presented by two texts on the same topic.	59-60
Range of Reading and Level of Text Complexity		
RI.2.10	By the end of year, read and comprehend informational texts, including history/social studies, science, and technical texts, in the grades 2–3 text complexity band proficiently, with scaffolding as needed at the high end of the range.	42-60

Common Core Reinforcement Activities: 2nd Grade Language

Reading Standards: Foundational Skills for Grade 2

Standard Number	Standard	Pages that Support
Phonics and Word Recognition		
RF.K-1.1	(Kindergarten and Grade 1 Standard)	*Not covered.*
RF.K-1.2	(Kindergarten and Grade 1 Standard)	*Not covered.*
RF.2.3	Know and apply grade-level phonics and word analysis skills in decoding words.	62-78
RF.2.3a	Distinguish long and short vowels when reading regularly spelled one-syllable words.	62, 63, 64, 65, 68
RF.2.3b	Know spelling-sound correspondences for additional common vowel teams.	66, 67, 68
RF.2.3c	Decode regularly spelled two-syllable words with long vowels.	64, 65, 68, 69
RF.2.3d	Decode words with common prefixes and suffixes.	69, 70, 71
RF.2.3e	Identify words with inconsistent but common spelling-sound correspondences.	72, 73, 74
RF.2.3f	Recognize and read grade-appropriate irregularly spelled words.	75, 76, 77, 78
Fluency		
RF.2.4	Read with sufficient accuracy and fluency to support comprehension.	*See note below.*
RF.2.4a	Read on-level text with purpose and understanding.	*See note below.*
RF.2.4b	Read on-level text orally with accuracy, appropriate rate, and expression on successive readings.	*See note below.*
RF.2.4c	Use context to confirm or self-correct word recognition and understanding, rereading as necessary.	*See note below.*

***Standard 4:** To nourish and assess fluency, it is necessary to listen to students read aloud and/or discuss with them the texts they read. Many pages in this book include stories, questions, or other texts that can be used to support or develop fluency and its connection to comprehension.*

College and Career Readiness Anchor Standards (CCRS) for Writing, Grades K-12

Standard Number	Standard	Pages that Support
Text Types and Purposes		
CCRA.W.1	Write arguments to support claims in an analysis of substantive topics or texts, using valid reasoning and relevant and sufficient evidence.	80-81, 82, 83
CCRA.W.2	Write informative/explanatory texts to examine and convey complex ideas and information clearly and accurately through the effective selection, organization, and analysis of content.	84, 85, 86
CCRA.W.3	Write narratives to develop real or imagined experiences or events using effective technique, well-chosen details, and well-structured event sequences.	87, 88
Production and Distribution of Writing		
CCRA.W.4	Produce clear and coherent writing in which the development, organization, and style are appropriate to task, purpose, and audience.	*Not covered. Begins in Grade 3.*
CCRA.W.5	Develop and strengthen writing as needed by planning, revising, editing, rewriting, or trying a new approach.	80-81, 82, 83, 84, 85, 86, 87, 88, 89, 90, 91, 92, 93, 94
CCRA.W.6	Use technology, including the Internet, to produce and publish writing and to interact and collaborate with others.	*See note below.*
Research to Build and Present Knowledge		
CCRA.W.7	Conduct short as well as more sustained research projects based on focused questions, demonstrating understanding of the subject under investigation.	92, 93, 94
CCRA.W.8	Gather relevant information from multiple print and digital sources, assess the credibility and accuracy of each source, and integrate the information while avoiding plagiarism.	92, 93, 94
CCRA.W.9	Draw evidence from literary or informational texts to support analysis, reflection, and research.	*Not covered. Begins in Grade 4.*
Range of Writing		
CCRA.W.10	Write routinely over extended time frames (time for research, reflection, and revision) and shorter time frames (a single sitting or a day or two) for a range of tasks, purposes, and audiences.	*Not covered. Begins in Grade 3.*

***Standard 6:** Use technology as a part of your approach for any of the activities in this writing section. Students can create, dictate, photograph, scan, enhance with art or color, or share any of the products they create as a part of these pages.*

Writing Standards for Grade 2

Standard Number	Standard	Pages that Support
Text Types and Purposes		
W.2.1	Write opinion pieces in which they introduce the topic or book they are writing about, state an opinion, supply reasons that support the opinion, use linking words (e.g., because, and, also) to connect opinion and reasons, and provide a concluding statement or section.	80-81, 82, 83
W.2.2	Write informative/explanatory texts in which they introduce a topic, use facts and definitions to develop points, and provide a concluding statement or section.	84, 85, 86
W.2.3	Write narratives in which they recount a well elaborated event or short sequence of events, include details to describe actions, thoughts, and feelings, use temporal words to signal event order, and provide a sense of closure.	87, 88
Production and Distribution of Writing		
W.2.4	Produce clear and coherent writing in which the development, organization, and style are appropriate to task, purpose, and audience.	*Not covered. Begins in Grade 3.*
W.2.5	With guidance and support from adults and peers, focus on a topic and strengthen writing as needed by revising and editing.	80-81, 82, 83, 84, 85, 86, 87, 88, 89, 90, 91, 92, 93, 94
W.2.6	With guidance and support from adults, use a variety of digital tools to produce and publish writing, including in collaboration with peers.	*See note below.*
Research to Build and Present Knowledge		
W.2.7	Participate in shared research and writing projects (e.g., read a number of books on a single topic to produce a report; record science observations).	92, 93, 94
W.2.8	Recall information from experiences or gather information from provided sources to answer a question.	92, 93, 94
W.2.9	Draw evidence from literary or informational texts to support analysis, reflection, and research.	*Not covered. Begins in Grade 4.*
Range of Writing		
W.2.10	Write routinely over extended time frames and shorter time frames for a range of tasks, purposes, and audiences.	*Not covered. Begins in Grade 3.*

Standard 6: *Use technology as a part of your approach for any of the activities in this writing section. Students can create, dictate, photograph, scan, enhance with art or color, or share any of the products they create as a part of these pages.*

College and Career Readiness Anchor Standards (CCRS) for Speaking and Listening, Grades K–12

Standard Number	Standard
Comprehension and Collaboration	
CCRA.SL.1	Prepare for and participate effectively in a range of conversations and collaborations with diverse partners, building on others' ideas and expressing their own clearly and persuasively.
CCRA.SL.2	Integrate and evaluate information presented in diverse media and formats, including visually, quantitatively, and orally.
CCRA.SL.3	Evaluate a speaker's point of view, reasoning, and use of evidence and rhetoric.
Presentation of Knowledge and Ideas	
CCRA.SL.4	Present information, findings, and supporting evidence such that listeners can follow the line of reasoning and the organization, development, and style are appropriate to task, purpose, and audience.
CCRA.SL.5	Make strategic use of digital media and visual displays of data to express information and enhance understanding of presentations.
CCRA.SL.6	Adapt speech to a variety of contexts and communicative tasks, demonstrating command of formal English when indicated or appropriate.

Speaking and Listening Standards: *The speaking and listening standards are not specifically addressed in this book. However, most pages can be used for conversation and collaboration. Teachers and parents are encouraged to use the activities in a sharing and discussion format. Many of the pages include visual information that students can include in the integration and evaluation of information.*

In addition, most of the texts and activities can be adapted to listening activities or can be used to support the listening and speaking standards.

Speaking and Listening Standards, Grade 2

Standard Number	Standard
Comprehension and Collaboration	
SL.2.1	Participate in collaborative conversations with diverse partners about *grade 2 topics and texts* with peers and adults in small and larger groups.
SL.2.1a	Follow agreed-upon rules for discussions (e.g., gaining the floor in respectful ways, listening to others with care, speaking one at a time about the topics and texts under discussion).
SL.2.1b	Build on others' talk in conversations by linking their comments to the remarks of others.
SL.2.1c	Ask for clarification and further explanation as needed about the topics and texts under discussion.
SL.2.2	Recount or describe key ideas or details from a text read aloud or information presented orally or through other media.
SL.2.3	Ask and answer questions about what a speaker says in order to clarify comprehension, gather additional information, or deepen understanding of a topic or issue.
Presentation of Knowledge and Ideas	
SL.2.4	Tell a story or recount an experience with appropriate facts and relevant, descriptive details, speaking audibly in coherent sentences.
SL.2.5	Create engaging audio recordings of stories or poems that demonstrate fluid reading; add drawings or other visual displays to stories or recounts of experiences when appropriate to clarify ideas, thoughts, and feelings.
SL.2.6	Produce complete sentences when appropriate to task and situation in order to provide requested detail or clarification. (See grade 2 Language standards 1 and 3 on pages 26 and 27 for specific expectations.)

Speaking and Listening Standards: *The speaking and listening standards are not specifically addressed in this book. However, most pages can be used for conversation and collaboration. Teachers and parents are encouraged to use the activities in a sharing and discussion format. Many of the pages include visual information that students can include in the integration and evaluation of information.*

In addition, most of the texts and activities can be adapted to listening activities or can be used to support the listening and speaking standards.

College and Career Readiness Anchor Standards (CCRS) for Language, Grades K-12

Standard Number	Standard	Pages that Support
Conventions of Standard English		
CCRA.L.1	Demonstrate command of the conventions of standard English grammar and usage when writing or speaking.	96, 97, 98-99, 100, 101, 102, 103, 104, 105
CCRA.L.2	Demonstrate command of the conventions of standard English capitalization, punctuation, and spelling when writing.	106, 107, 108, 109, 110, 111
Knowledge of Language		
CCRA.L.3	Apply knowledge of language to understand how language functions in different contexts, to make effective choices for meaning or style, and to comprehend more fully when reading or listening.	112
Vocabulary Acquisition and Use		
CCRA.L.4	Determine or clarify the meaning of unknown and multiple-meaning words and phrases by using context clues, analyzing meaningful word parts, and consulting general and specialized reference materials, as appropriate.	113, 114, 115, 116, 117, 118, 119, 120, 121, 122, 123, 124-125, 126
CCRA.L.5	Demonstrate understanding of figurative language, word relationships, and nuances in word meanings.	123, 126
CCRA.L.6	Acquire and use accurately a range of general academic and domain-specific words and phrases sufficient for reading, writing, speaking, and listening at the college and career readiness level; demonstrate independence in gathering vocabulary knowledge when encountering an unknown term important to comprehension or expression.	50, 52, 53, 113, 114, 115, 116, 117, 118, 119, 120, 121, 122, 123, 124-125, 126

Language Standards for Grade 2

Standard Number	Standard	Pages that Support
Conventions of Standard English		
L.2.1	Demonstrate command of the conventions of standard English grammar and usage when writing or speaking.	96-112
L.2.1a	Use collective nouns.	112
L.2.1b	Form and use frequently occurring irregular plural nouns.	97
L.2.1c	Use reflexive pronouns.	100
L.2.1d	Form and use the past tense of frequently occurring irregular verbs.	98–99
L.2.1e	Use adjectives and adverbs, and choose between them, depending on what is to be modified.	101, 102
L.2.1f	Produce, expand, and rearrange complete simple and compound sentences.	103, 104, 105
L.2.2	Demonstrate command of the conventions of standard English capitalization, punctuation, and spelling when writing.	106-111, 112
L.2.2a	Capitalize holidays, product names, and geographic names.	106
L.2.2b	Use commas in greetings and closing of letters.	107
L.2.2c	Use an apostrophe to form contractions and frequently occurring possessives.	108
L.2.2d	Generalize learned spelling patterns when writing words.	109, 110, 111
L.2.2e	Consult reference materials, including beginning dictionaries, as needed to check and correct spellings.	111
Knowledge of Language		
L.2.3	Use knowledge of language and its conventions when writing, speaking, reading, or listening.	112
L.2.3a	Compare formal and informal uses of English.	112

Language standards continue on the next page.

Language Standards for Grade 2, continued

Standard Number	Standard	Pages that Support
Vocabulary Acquisition and Use		
L.2.4	Determine or clarify the meaning of unknown and multiple-meaning word and phrases based on grade 2 reading and content, choosing flexibly from a range of strategies.	113-120
L.2.4a	Use sentence-level context as a clue to the meaning of a word or phrase.	113, 114, 115, 116, 120
L.2.4b	Determine the meaning of the new word formed when a known affix is added to a known word (e.g., *happy/unhappy; tell/retell*).	116, 118
L.2.4c	Use a known root word as a clue to the meaning of an unknown word with the same root (e.g., *addition/additional*).	116, 118
L.2.4d	Use knowledge of the meaning of individual words to predict the meaning of compound words.	119
L.2.4e	Use glossaries or beginning dictionaries, both print and digital, to determine or clarify the precise meaning of key words and phrases.	120
L.2.5	Demonstrate understanding of word relationships and nuances in word meanings.	117, 121-126
L.2.5a	Identify real-life connections between words and their use (e.g., describe foods that are *spicy* or *juicy*).	121, 122
L.2.5b	Distinguish shades of meaning among closely related verbs (e.g., *toss, throw, hurl*) and closely related adjectives (e.g, *thin, slender, skinny, scrawny*).	123, 126
L.2.6	Use words and phrases acquired through conversations, reading and being read to, and responding to texts, including using adjectives and adverbs to describe (e.g., *When other kids are happy that makes me happy*).	124, 125

—

READING

LITERATURE

Grade 2

Shopping List:
popcorn
apples
pizza
cookies
potato chips
lemonade
sandwiches
grapes
carrots
paper plates
napkins
watermelon

Being Lost Is No Fun

Suzie and Becky wandered away from the group.
Something happened that they did not plan!

Read the story to find out what happened.

Suzie and Becky are so frightened.

They have lost their friends.

They don't know where they are.

They hear a roaring noise.

Now they are even more frightened.

Suzie sees a big furry shape.

Becky sees two big red eyes
staring at them.

They run fast.

They want to get away from the
roaring sound and red eyes!

1. Circle the main idea of the story.
   a. Two friends run fast.
   b. Two friends are planning a camping trip.
   c. Suzie and Becky get lost in the woods and become very frightened.

2. Draw in the circle what you think frightened the friends.

3. What did they hear and see
   that frightened them?

   _____

   _____

   _____

   _____

Name _____

School in a Tree

Read the poem about the school in a tree. Follow the directions in the box to finish the picture.

Circle the sentences that tell what the students learn.

> Climb the steps and take a seat
> In a school with no walls or door.
> Do your math in rain or heat.
> Dry your art on the open wood floor.
>
> Science is everywhere you look—
> In the sky and in the trees.
> Read a story from your book
> While you watch the clouds and bees.

Draw: a clock on the tree
a book on the teacher's desk
an apple on the teacher's desk
a spider on the railing

Put an X in the box that tells the main idea of the poem.

☐ Students get thirsty while they study.

☐ At this school, students learn in the outdoors.

☐ The schoolwork is hard.

Name

Key Ideas, Details
Common Core Reinforcement Activities: 2nd Grade Language

A Deep-Sea Scare

Benjy made up this deep-sea picture story.

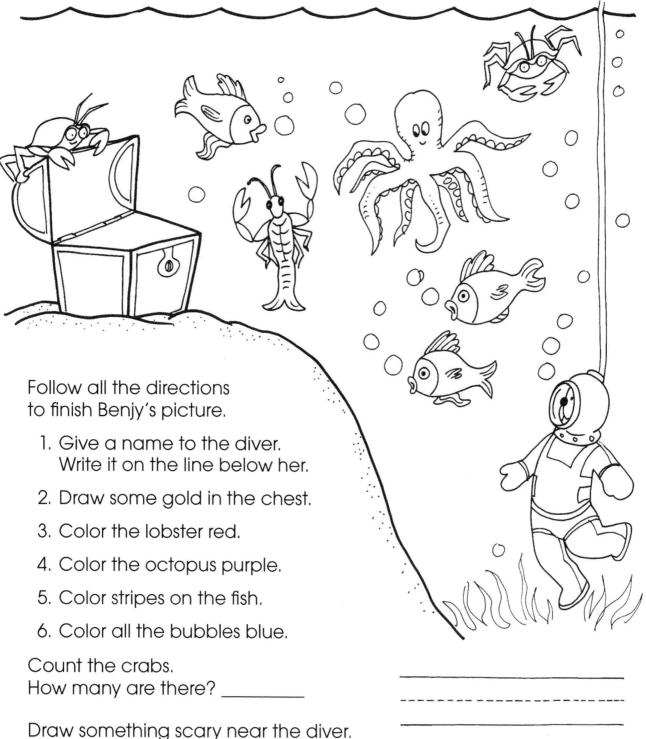

Follow all the directions
to finish Benjy's picture.

1. Give a name to the diver.
   Write it on the line below her.

2. Draw some gold in the chest.

3. Color the lobster red.

4. Color the octopus purple.

5. Color stripes on the fish.

6. Color all the bubbles blue.

Count the crabs.
How many are there? _____

Draw something scary near the diver.

Name the diver.

Name

Key Ideas, Details
Common Core Reinforcement Activities: 2nd Grade Language

Copyright © 2014 World Book, Inc./
Incentive Publications, Chicago, IL

Silly Sentences

Suzie Squirrel scribbles silly sentences. Students at Happy Hollow School like to read them!

Read the sentences and answer the questions.

Say these seven silly sentences.

1. Benjy, the brown beaver, bounced balls.

2. Funny Flossie Frog found fifty-five fleas.

3. Polly Porcupine planned a pickle party.

4. Who sipped sodas with Suzie Squirrel?

5. Bubba Bunny brought Bobby a big bag of books.

6. Did Chippy Chipmunk chop chunks of cheese?

7. Randall Rat raced around behind Ricki Raccoon.

A. Which sentences are about food? _____

B. Who chased someone? _____

C. Who caught some bugs? _____

D. What did you learn about Benjy? _____

_____

_____

Name _____

Key Ideas, Details
Common Core Reinforcement Activities: 2nd Grade Language

The Lion and the Mouse

Read the story about how a tiny mouse helped a huge lion.

Yum

A long time ago in the jungle, a lion caught a tiny mouse for a snack. The mouse cried, "Please don't eat me! If you let me go, I promise I will help you some day!"

The lion thought it was funny that such a small thing could help him. While he was laughing, the mouse escaped and ran away.

Many days later, the big, powerful lion was caught in a trap. The mouse was far away, but he heard the lion's roar. He ran and found the trapped lion.

"I am here to help you!" cried the mouse. The lion did not laugh. The tiny mouse chewed through the ropes. In no time, the lion was free. From that day on, the lion and the mouse were best friends.

1. Tell someone this story in your own words. Write the name of the person who listened to your story.

_____

2. This story is a fable. A fable teaches a lesson. Circle the letter of the lesson this fable teaches.

    a. Lions sometimes get trapped.

    b. Even a small creature can be helpful.

    c. A lion should never eat a mouse.

    d. A mouse is smarter than a lion.

Name _____

The Tale of the Elephant's Nose

How did the elephant get such a long nose?

Here is a story that has been told for many years!

It is called a folk tale.

Decide if you think it is true!

A long time ago, elephants had short noses. One day, an elephant child changed that. The curious young elephant wanted to know what a crocodile eats for dinner.

So he went to the green Limpopo River to find out. There he found a long crocodile. "I have been looking for you, crocodile. Please tell me what you have for dinner."

"Come closer and I will whisper the answer, little elephant!"

The elephant got closer. The crocodile's big teeth caught him by the nose. The elephant pulled. The crocodile pulled. The elephant's nose kept stretching and stretching.

At last, the crocodile let go. The elephant's nose hurt! He waited for it to shrink. But it never did. That's how the elephant got a long trunk.

1. Tell someone this story in your own words. Write the name of the person who listened to your story.

   _____

2. What is the main idea of this story? _____

   _____

   _____

Name

Key Ideas, Details, Characters
Common Core Reinforcement Activities: 2nd Grade Language

The Big Game

The Happy Hollow School soccer team wins lots of games. The school is proud of the team. Read the news report about the latest game. Then answer the questions.

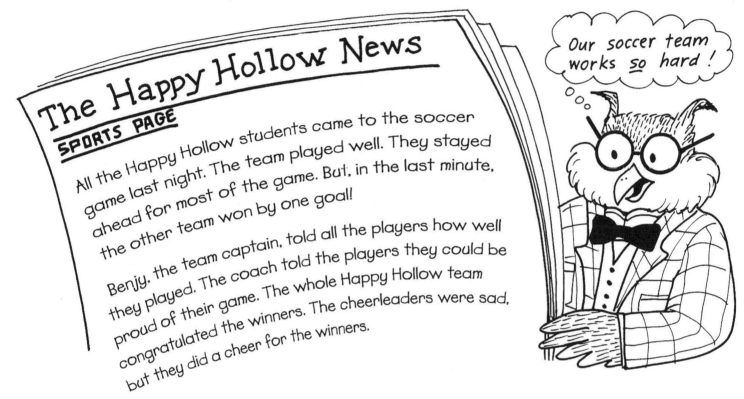

The Happy Hollow News

SPORTS PAGE

All the Happy Hollow students came to the soccer game last night. The team played well. They stayed ahead for most of the game. But, in the last minute, the other team won by one goal!

Benjy, the team captain, told all the players how well they played. The coach told the players they could be proud of their game. The whole Happy Hollow team congratulated the winners. The cheerleaders were sad, but they did a cheer for the winners.

Our soccer team works so hard!

1. How did the players on the Happy Hollow team act when they lost the game?

   _____

   _____

   _____

2. What did the coach do when the team lost?

   _____

   _____

3. How did the cheerleaders act when the team lost?

   _____

   _____

   _____

Name _____

The Shopping Trip

It's time to shop for the school picnic. Read about Owl's shopping trip. Then answer the questions.

Shopping List:
popcorn
apples
pizza
cookies
potato chips
lemonade
sandwiches
grapes
carrots
paper plates
napkins
watermelon

Owl made a list of food to buy. It was on a very small piece of paper. He put it in his pocket. He went shopping. He bought popcorn, apples, and pizza. Then he went home. "Oh, where is the rest of the food?" he thought.

He went back to the store. He bought watermelon and napkins. Then he went home. "Something is wrong," he said.

Owl made a bigger list. It was as big as the shopping cart. He went back to the store. This time he did not miss anything on the list.

1. What was Owl's problem? (Circle one.)
   a. He had too much junk food on his list.
   b. He did not make a list.
   c. His list was too small, and it was in his pocket.
   d. He bought the wrong foods.

2. What did Owl do to solve his problem?

   _____

   _____

   _____

   _____

   _____

Name _____

Key Ideas, Details, Characters
Common Core Reinforcement Activities: 2nd Grade Language

Classroom Rules

Teacher Wise Owl made the classroom rules into a song. On the first day of school, he sang the song to the students. Read the song. Answer the questions.

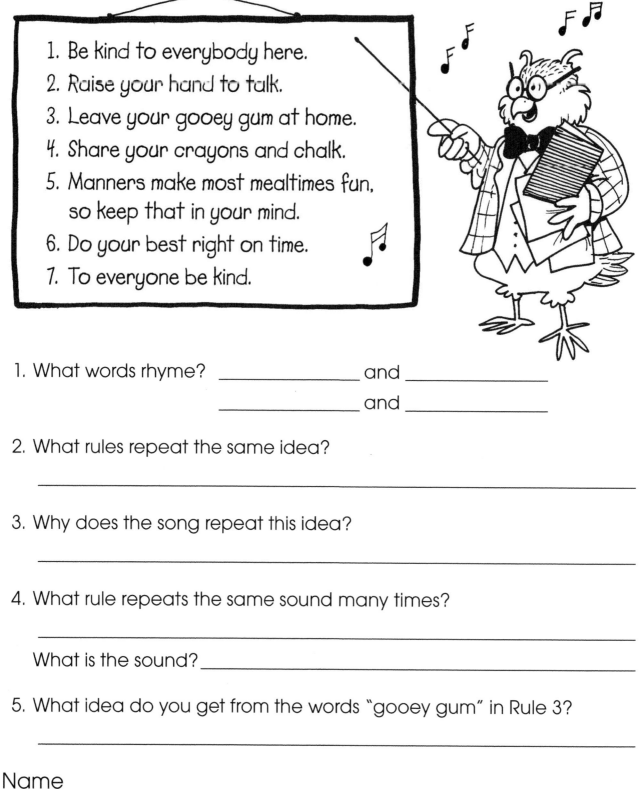

1. Be kind to everybody here.
2. Raise your hand to talk.
3. Leave your gooey gum at home.
4. Share your crayons and chalk.
5. Manners make most mealtimes fun, so keep that in your mind.
6. Do your best right on time.
7. To everyone be kind.

1. What words rhyme? _____ and _____

   _____ and _____

2. What rules repeat the same idea?

   _____

3. Why does the song repeat this idea?

   _____

4. What rule repeats the same sound many times?

   _____

   What is the sound? _____

5. What idea do you get from the words "gooey gum" in Rule 3?

   _____

Name _____

School Supplies

Peek inside Bella Blue Jay's closet.

Read the sentences.

Then answer the questions below the closet.

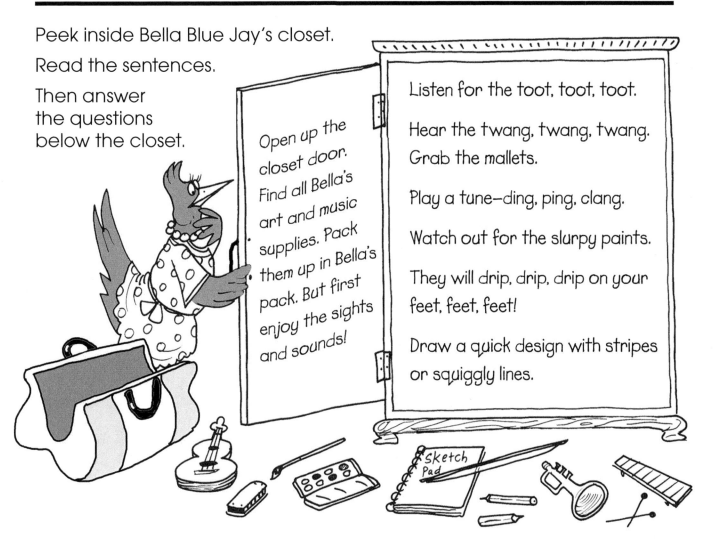

Open up the closet door. Find all Bella's art and music supplies. Pack them up in Bella's pack. But first enjoy the sights and sounds!

Listen for the toot, toot, toot.

Hear the twang, twang, twang. Grab the mallets.

Play a tune—ding, ping, clang.

Watch out for the slurpy paints.

They will drip, drip, drip on your feet, feet, feet!

Draw a quick design with stripes or squiggly lines.

1. What words give the feeling of music? Circle them with a red crayon.

2. What words give the idea of art? Circle them with a blue crayon.

3. Why do you think the writer repeated some words?

_____

_____

_____

_____

_____

Name

Words, Rhythm, Meaning
Common Core Reinforcement Activities: 2nd Grade Language

The Great Hit

Pedro plays baseball for his school team.

The story is about his greatest hit.

Read it. Then follow the directions below the story.

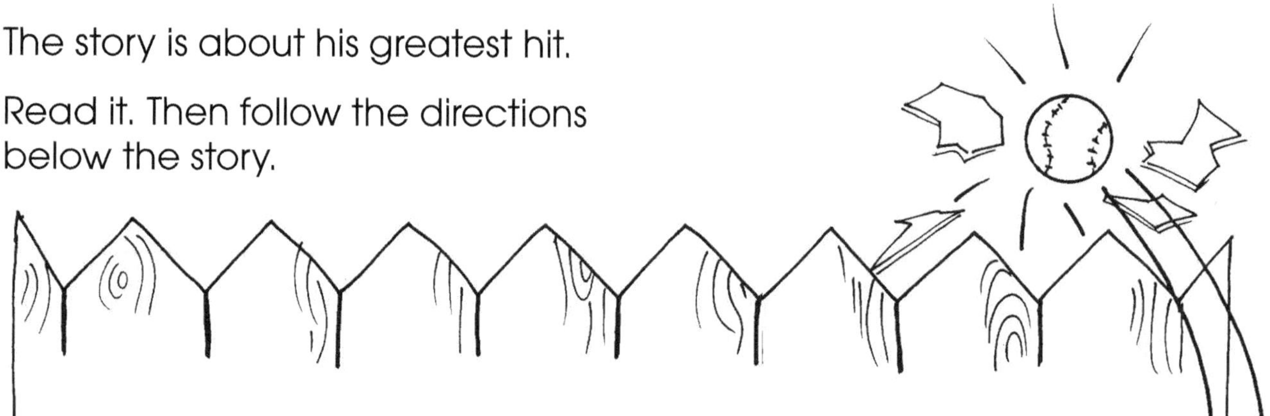

The Great Hit

Pedro wanted this to be his best game. He practiced hitting the ball every day.

"Today I will hit a home run," he said.

He was right. WHACK! Pedro got an amazing hit. The ball soared high up into the air. It sailed over the fence. It went right into Bella Blue Jay's window!

Pedro got a home run.

In your own words, tell someone how you would finish each sentence.

1. To begin, the story tells that _____ .

2. The main thing that happens in the story is _____ .

3. The story ends by telling that _____ .

Name _____

Math Mix-Up

When Pedro explained the math assignment to Flossie, things got mixed up.

What did Pedro mean to say?

Fix the mixed up sentences. Write each one correctly.

1. addition subtraction we studying are and

_____

_____

2. the are page 21 on problems

_____

_____

_____

3. problems 22 are there all in

_____

_____

_____

4. assignment due the tomorrow is

_____

_____

_____

5. study together let's

_____

_____

_____

I don't get it!

Text Structure
Common Core Reinforcement Activities: 2nd Grade Language

Cloud Watching

Flossie Frog is feeling a bit lazy today. She is watching clouds instead of doing homework.

Her thoughts are on the clouds. Read all her thoughts.

Flossie has two different views about her cloud watching. Discuss these with other students.

What do the Letter **A** thoughts show? _____

_____

What do the Letter **B** thoughts show? _____

_____

Name _____

A Picnic Memory

This picture was taken at the Happy Hollow School picnic.

Study the picture for a minute. Then cover it with paper.

Complete the sentences.

Then uncover the picture to check your answers.

1. (How many?) _____ students are enjoying the picnic.

2. The fruit basket is filled with _____ .

3. There are three _____ in the stream.

4. A _____ is perched on the lily pad.

5. Three students are playing _____ .

6. There will be plenty of _____ to drink.

7. A good title for this picture would be _____

_____

Name _____

Copyright © 2014 World Book, Inc./
Incentive Publications, Chicago, IL

35

Information from Illustrations
Common Core Reinforcement Activities: 2nd Grade Language

Dressed for Drama

These students are dressed for the class play.
The name of the play is *The Forest Queen*.

Read all the clues to find out which character each will play.
Write the correct name below each creature.

The Forest Queen

_____   _____

_____   _____

_____

CLUES

The queen wears a crown.

The prince wears sneakers.

The princess loves jewelry.

The thief stands
next to the prince.

The queen's maid carries
the queen's pillow.

1. Which character has the most
   interesting costume?

   _____

   _____

2. What is interesting about the costume
   you chose?

   _____

   _____

Name

Talent Show

Preparations for The Happy Hollow Talent Show are underway.
Ms. Bella Blue Jay is in charge.

Help Ms. Bella match each student with his or her talents.

Draw a line from each picture to the matching sentence.

Suki Skunk reads poetry.

Flossie Frog sings opera.

Benjy Beaver plays the harp.

Pedro Porcupine tap dances.

Suzie Squirrel dances ballet.

Becky Bunny is a gymnast.

Ricki Raccoon plays the harmonica.

What talent looks most difficult?

Write the student's name.

Name

Information from Illustrations
Common Core Reinforcement Activities: 2nd Grade Language

Lost Name Tags

The teacher has a problem. All the students' name tags are lost.

Read the clues to help the teacher find out the students' names.

Write each student's name on his or her name tag.

The student with the big hair bow is named Suzie.

Pedro has on tennis shoes.

Ricki is sitting next to Pedro.

Flossie always looks as if she is about to fly away.

The lunch box belongs to Benjy.

You never see Becky without a book.

Sammy sits next to Suzie.

Name

Playground Fun

Read about the playground fun.

Compare this with the next page (page 40).

Answer the questions on page 40.

1. Suzie loves the slide.
   She closes her eyes
   and enjoys the ride.

2. The seesaw goes
   up and down. Pedro
   and Sammy balance
   carefully on the ends.

3. Silly Flossie likes to swing while
   she licks her lollipop.
   Is this a good idea?

Use with page 40.

Name

Compare, Contrast
Common Core Reinforcement Activities: 2nd Grade Language

Playground Fun, continued

Read about the playground fun. Compare this with page 39.

4. Open your eyes quickly now!
   Watch where you will land.
   You're headed into mucky muck,
   But you think it is sand!

5. Sammy just slipped off his seat
   But Pedro, do not worry!
   You can keep from crashing down
   If you jump off in a hurry!

6. Silly Flossie swings so high
   While she licks her lollipop.
   Flossie, you just might choke
   If you don't decide to stop!

Talk about these questions with your classmates:

1. How are the stories for the same pictures on pages 39 and 40 like each other?

2. What is different about the stories on pages 39 and 40?

Use with page 39.

Name

Compare, Contrast
Common Core Reinforcement Activities: 2nd Grade Language

40

Copyright © 2014 World Book, Inc./
Incentive Publications, Chicago, IL

READING

INFORMATIONAL TEXT

Grade 2

Forest News, July 10

Crab Completes Difficult Climb

Forest News, July 10

Raccoon Caught Stealing Food

Picnic Tummy Aches

At the picnic, the students ate too much food.
Now they all have tummy aches.

The graph shows how much
of each food they ate.

Read the graph to answer the questions.

Circle the correct answers:

1. Which food was eaten the most?
   cookies   sandwiches

2. How many sandwiches were eaten?
   20   10   26

3. Which food was eaten the least?
   pizza   chips   sandwiches

4. How many pizzas were eaten?
   8   12   10   9

5. How many jugs of lemonade
   did the animals drink?
   26   9   20

6. How many cookies were eaten?
   10   8   26   20

7. The animals ate only 8:
   sandwiches   pizzas   cookies

8. How many bags of chips were eaten?
   9   10   20

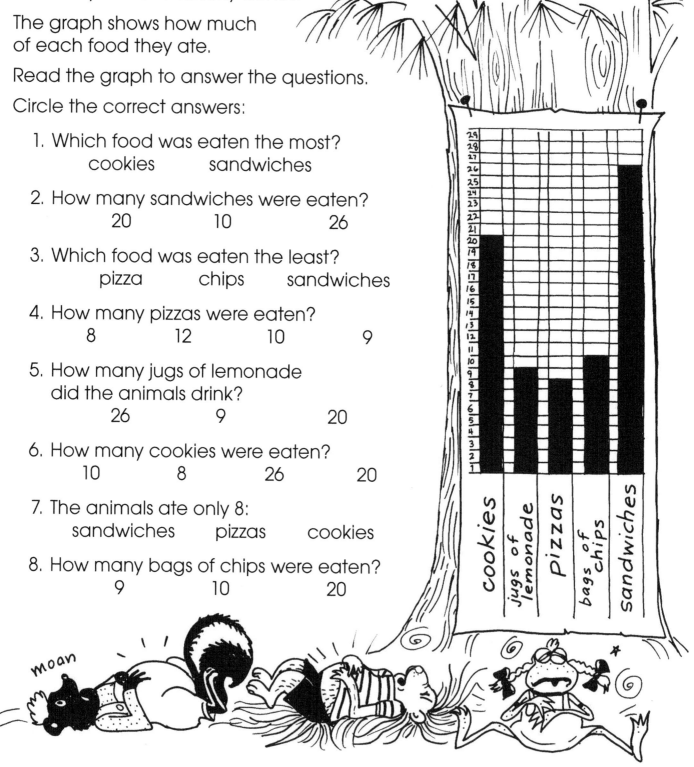

Key Ideas, Details
Common Core Reinforcement Activities: 2nd Grade Language

A Report on Gilas

The Gila monster is not really a monster!

Becky wrote this report for science class.
Read her report and find out about Gila monsters.

Circle the correct answers.

Gila Monsters   by Becky Bunny

Gilas are big lizards.

They live in North America in hot places.

They can live a long time without food.

They hibernate in winter.

This Gila has a big head and a thick tail.

It is black with pink and yellow spots.

Gila monsters move very slowly.

1. What is a Gila monster?	snake	lizard	turtle
2. What kind of tail does it have?	curly	thin	thick
3. What colors are its spots?	red	pink and yellow	purple
4. How does it move?	rapidly	in circles	slowly
5. Where do Gila monsters live?	Asia	North America	Africa

Name

Copyright © 2014 World Book, Inc./
Incentive Publications, Chicago, IL

Key Ideas, Details
Common Core Reinforcement Activities: 2nd Grade Language

Detective's Helper

Rufus is trying to solve some mysteries.

Be his helper.

Read the clues and answer the questions.

1. A castle is on fire.
   A dragon gallops away from the castle.
   What caused the fire?

   _____

   _____

2. The cookie jar was full, but now it's empty.
   Muddy paw prints cover the kitchen floor.
   What happened to the cookies?

   _____

   _____

3. Seven scorpions were asleep in the jar.
   A scream is heard in the next room.
   What happened?

   _____

   _____

4. The garbage can is full.
   Reggie Raccoon is nearby.
   What might happen next?

   _____

   _____

Name

To Market, to Market!

The Happy Hollow students love Farmer Joe.

Solve the riddles to find out what they buy from the market.

Write the word that finishes each poem.

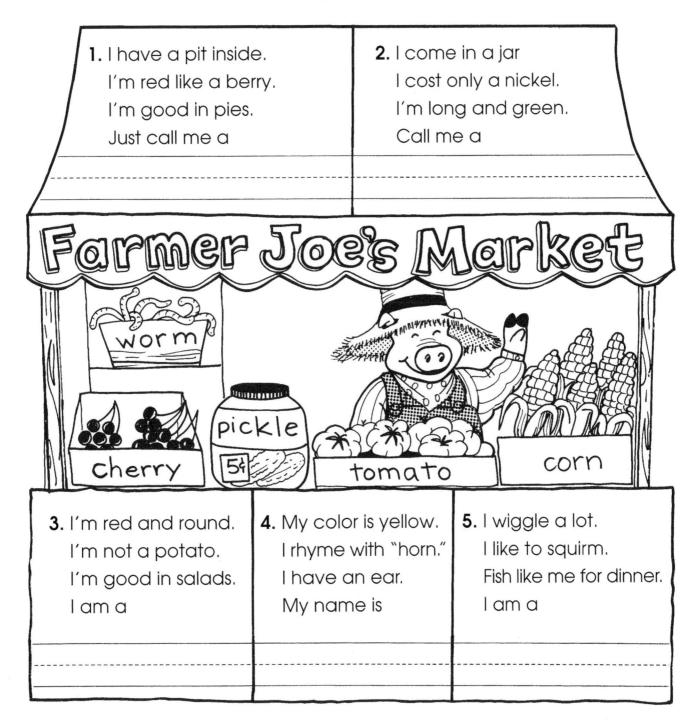

1. I have a pit inside.
I'm red like a berry.
I'm good in pies.
Just call me a

2. I come in a jar
I cost only a nickel.
I'm long and green.
Call me a

worm

pickle 5¢

cherry

tomato

corn

3. I'm red and round.
I'm not a potato.
I'm good in salads.
I am a

4. My color is yellow.
I rhyme with "horn."
I have an ear.
My name is

5. I wiggle a lot.
I like to squirm.
Fish like me for dinner.
I am a

Name

Copyright © 2014 World Book, Inc./
Incentive Publications, Chicago, IL

Key Ideas, Details
Common Core Reinforcement Activities: 2nd Grade Language

Body Parts You Can't See

Read about important parts that are inside your body.

A skeleton is inside your body. It is made of bones.

You have bones in your head, arms and fingers, legs and toes. You have hip bones and bones around your chest.

What are bones good for? They give your body shape. They protect everything inside, such as your heart, brain, and stomach. Without bones, you would not be able to stand up or move!

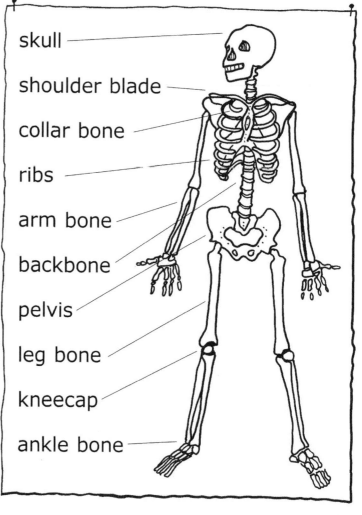

skull

shoulder blade

collar bone

ribs

arm bone

backbone

pelvis

leg bone

kneecap

ankle bone

Draw a line to the main idea for . . .

1. the whole passage about bones

2. the first part

3. the second part

a. There are bones in every part of your body.

b. Bones protect your insides and help you move.

c. A body needs its skeleton!

Name _____

Something's Missing

Something is missing from the plants in Abby's pictures.

Write the correct word in each box below.

Then draw the plant parts to finish both pictures.

1. The [   ] hold the plant in the ground. They take in water and nutrients from the soil.

2. The [   ] holds up the leaves. It carries water and nutrients to the plant.

3. The [   ] use air, water, and sunlight to make food for the plant.

4. The [   ] is the place where fruits and seeds form in many plants.

5. The [   ] is where seeds form in plants such as pine or fir trees.

Name

Connections to Content-Area Topics
Common Core Reinforcement Activities: 2nd Grade Language

Which Happened First?

Look at the giant timeline of U.S. history!

Use it to answer the questions. Circle the correct answer.

1. Which happened **first**?
    a. Telephone invented
    b. First airplane ride
    c. Abe Lincoln elected

2. Which happened **first**?
    a. Women get right to vote
    b. Gold discovered
    c. Kennedy elected

3. Which happened **last**?
    a. U.S. is born
    b. Pilgrims arrive
    c. Washington elected

4. Which happened **first**?
    a. Statue of Liberty arrives
    b. Telephone invented
    c. First moon walk

5. Which happened **first**?
    a. First moon walk
    b. Statue of Liberty arrives
    c. U.S. 200th birthday

6. Which happened **last**?
    a. Kennedy elected
    b. Lincoln elected
    c. Washington elected

1620	**Pilgrims arrive**
1776	**The U.S. is born**
1789	**George Washington becomes first president**
1848	**Gold discovered in California**
1860	**Abe Lincoln elected 16th U.S. president**
1876	**Telephone invented**
1884	**France gives U.S. the Statue of Liberty**
1903	**First airplane ride**
1920	**Women get the right to vote**
1960	**Kennedy elected president**
1969	**First moon walk**
1976	**200th birthday for U.S.**

Name

Who Can You Call?

Help!

There are many community services that can help you with different needs.
Which one should you call for each problem below?
Draw a line to match each need with the place or service that meets it.

1. You need help finding a fact for your history homework.

2. You see a fire out your window.

3. You find a lost child in the street.

4. You want to use the park picnic area for your soccer team party.

5. You see water gushing out of a pipe in the street.

6. Someone has been badly hurt.

7. You need to find a zip code.

8. Your garbage has not been picked up for three weeks.

9. There is a dangerous dog loose in your neighborhood.

10. The electricity has gone out on your street.

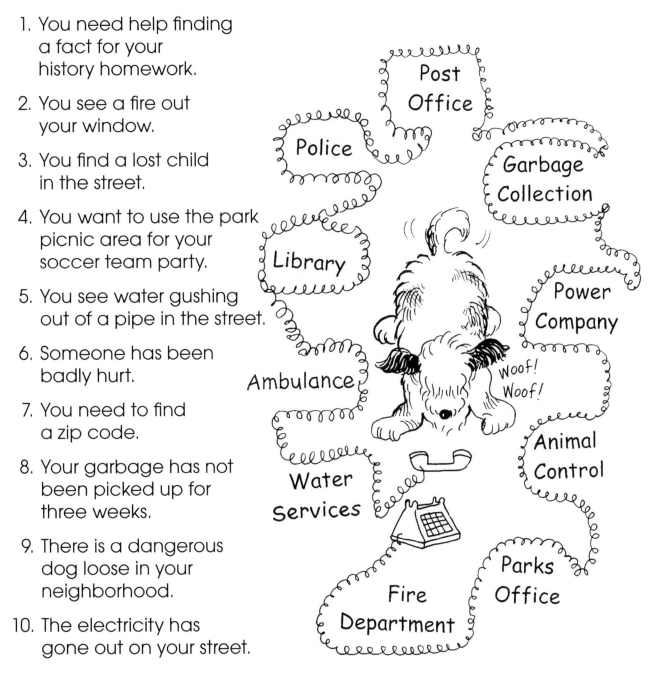

Name

Academic Vocabulary
Common Core Reinforcement Activities: 2nd Grade Language

How Those Animals Behave!

Animals do some very strange and interesting things. What they do is called **animal behavior**. Here are some kinds of animal behavior.

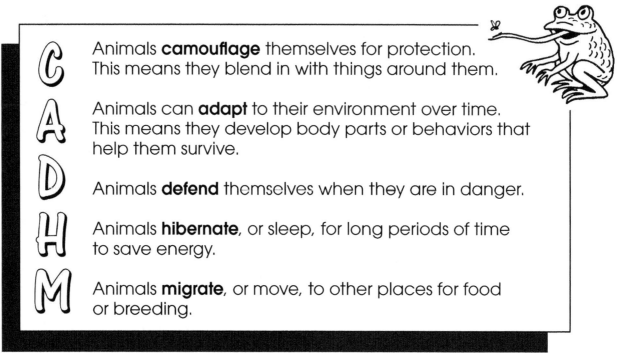

C Animals **camouflage** themselves for protection. This means they blend in with things around them.

A Animals can **adapt** to their environment over time. This means they develop body parts or behaviors that help them survive.

D Animals **defend** themselves when they are in danger.

H Animals **hibernate**, or sleep, for long periods of time to save energy.

M Animals **migrate**, or move, to other places for food or breeding.

What behavior does each picture show? Write one of the big letters beneath the picture. Be ready to explain your choice.

1. _____

2. _____

3. _____

4. _____

5. _____

6. _____

7. _____

8. _____

Name _____

Picture Stories to Finish

What happens next? Draw a picture in box 3 to show what you think happens next. Write your own caption beneath the box.

Becky wants
some honey.

The bee hive
is full of honey.

Two friends both
want the same ball.

The teacher
comes running.

Name

Text Features
Common Core Reinforcement Activities: 2nd Grade Language

What Do Bees Know?

Bees get their food from flowers. They know just what each part of the flower is for!

Read about the flower parts. Find the bee that is visiting each part. Write the bee's letter next to the number.

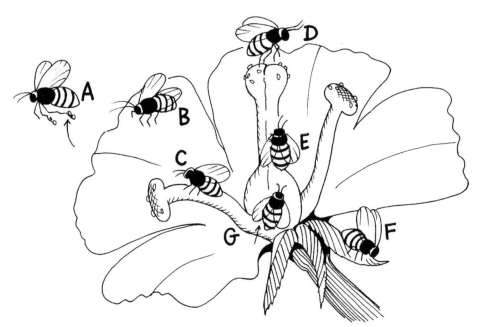

_____ 1. The bright **petals** protect the flower and attract bees.

_____ 2. The **sepals** are at the bottom of the petals. They protect the flower before it opens.

_____ 3. The tall **pistil** in the center contains a round ovary at the bottom.

_____ 4. The **ovary** is where seeds grow.

_____ 5. The **stigma** is the sticky top of the pistil. Grains of pollen stick to it. They send tubes down into the ovary to help seeds grow.

_____ 6. The tall **stamens** stick out from near the ovary. They produce pollen grains.

_____ 7. Grains of **pollen** help to produce new seeds. Pollen sticks to bees. They carry the pollen to other flowers.

8. Why did the author write this? Talk about it with your classmates.

Name

Job Search

GOODS
Some people work to grow
or make the things we buy and use!
I am visiting those workers today.
Color my path RED.

SERVICES
Some people work
to do things for other people.
These things are called services.
I am visiting those workers today.
Color my path GREEN.

gardener

police officer

baker   mayor

automaker   banker   waiter

builder   cook   baseball player

librarian   artist   farmer

plumber   grocery store clerk   animal trainer

president   shoemaker

tent maker

firefighter   janitor

auto salesperson

piano teacher

doctor

Why did the author write this? Talk about it with your classmates.

Name

Author's Purpose
Common Core Reinforcement Activities: 2nd Grade Language

Follow the Parade!

Every year the circus comes to Berry Town.

Maybe the parade will pass by Noah's house.

Follow the route of the parade on the map.

Use the **map key** to answer the questions about the parade.

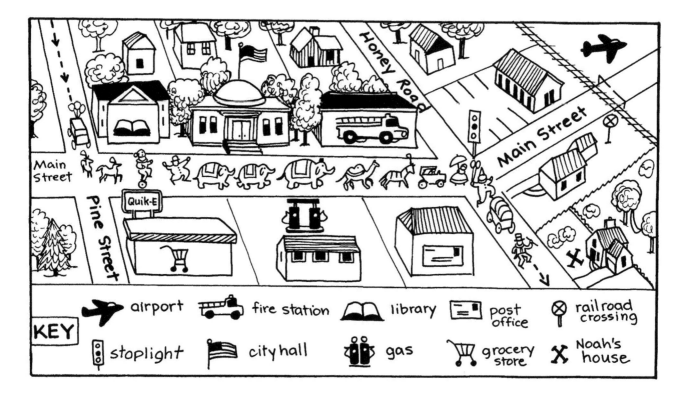

1. Will the parade pass the post office?   yes   no

2. How many stoplights will the parade pass? _____

3. Is the airport near the library?   yes   no

4. How many different streets will the parade be on? _____

5. Will the parade pass the airport?   yes   no

6. Will the parade pass Noah's house?   yes   no

Name

Circus, Circus

The circus is coming to Happy Hollow.

Look at the pictures of all the circus acts.

Then answer the questions.

Circle your answers. Be ready to explain them.
Use information from the pictures.

1. What part of the show do you like best? Tell why.

elephant tricks	lion tamer	clown	trapeze
dog tricks	tightrope	fire eater	

2. What job do you think is the most dangerous? Tell why.

lion tamer	trapeze artist	tightrope walker
clown	fire eater	elephant trainer

3. What animal do you think has the hardest job? Tell why.

lion	cat	dog	elephant	bear

Name

Who Gets the Milk?

Here comes the milk truck to the Moptown Trailer Park!
Follow the directions to figure out who will get milk.

1. In the trailers east and west of the milk truck, water is the only drink. Color these brown.

2. Milk is delivered to the trailer northeast of the truck. Color this trailer green.

3. Honey is the favorite drink in the trailer south of the truck. Color this trailer yellow.

4. The animal in the trailer southeast of the truck drinks only soda pop. Color this trailer orange.

5. The trailer north of the truck orders cactus juice. Draw a green box around it.

6. Milk is delivered to the trailers northwest and southwest of the truck. Color them red.

Name

Rafting on the River

Becky's friends sent her pictures of their rafting trip. She wrote a story about the pictures.

Answer the questions at the bottom.

**We are in a raft.
We are starting down the river.**

This is fun! The river is wild.

Oops! We tip over. We get very wet.

We are three wet, tired dogs.

1. Why did the dogs get wet? _____

_____

_____

_____

2. Why were the dogs tired? _____

_____

_____

_____

Name _____

Supporting Reasons
Common Core Reinforcement Activities: 2nd Grade Language

Benjy's List

Benjy writes a list of some things he has learned about his new school. He also writes some of his thoughts.

Read what Benjy wrote. Answer the questions.

Happy Hollow School is such fun.

The soccer team is very good.

I can't wait to get my soccer equipment.

There are many different subjects.

Students go on lots of field trips.

The library is huge.

I am glad it has a lot of science books.

My favorite teacher is the art teacher.

This is a great school.

1. Does Benjy feel good about his new school? _____
   Use red to circle parts that explain your answer.

2. Does Benjy like science?_____
   Use blue to circle the part that explains your answer.

3. Do students learn things away from school? _____
   Use green to circle the part that explains your answer.

4. What subjects does Benjy like?_____

   _____

   Use purple to circle parts that explain your answer.

Name

Disappearing Dinosaurs

Dinosaurs roamed Earth a long time ago.

They are extinct now, so it is such fun to learn about them.

Read about five different dinosaurs on this page and the next page (page 60). Answer the question at the bottom of each page.

Brachiosaurus

The *Brachiosaurus* was one of the biggest dinosaurs.

It had a long neck and walked on four legs.

Part of its name means "lizard."

This plant-eating creature is a very popular dinosaur.

Triceratops

What a huge skull this dinosaur had!

Its name means "three-horned face." The horns were used as weapons. A fancy-looking collar was at the top of its head.

Triceratops dinosaurs ate plants and lived in herds.

How are these dinosaur texts like the texts on the next page?

Discuss this with your classmates.

Use with page 60.

Name

Disappearing Dinosaurs, continued

Read about the five different dinosaurs on this page and page 59. Answer the question at the bottom of each page.

The *Troodon*
Was really rather small.

But its large brain made it one of
The smartest dinosaurs of all.

Troodon

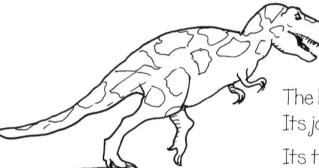

Tyrannosaurus Rex

The huge *T. Rex* ate lots of meat.
Its jaws were very strong.

Its teeth and claws were sharp.
No one stayed near it for long!

This dinosaur looks like an elephant,
With bony plates along its spine.

With no front teeth, some soft green plants
Made a meal that suited it fine.

Stegosaurus

How are these dinosaur texts different from the texts on the other page?

Discuss this with your classmates.

Use with page 59.

Name

60

READING

FOUNDATIONAL SKILLS

Grade 2

An A-B-C Adventure

Molly Mouse is having a great sea adventure.

Connect the dots in A-B-C order to find out about it.

Say each word aloud as you read it.

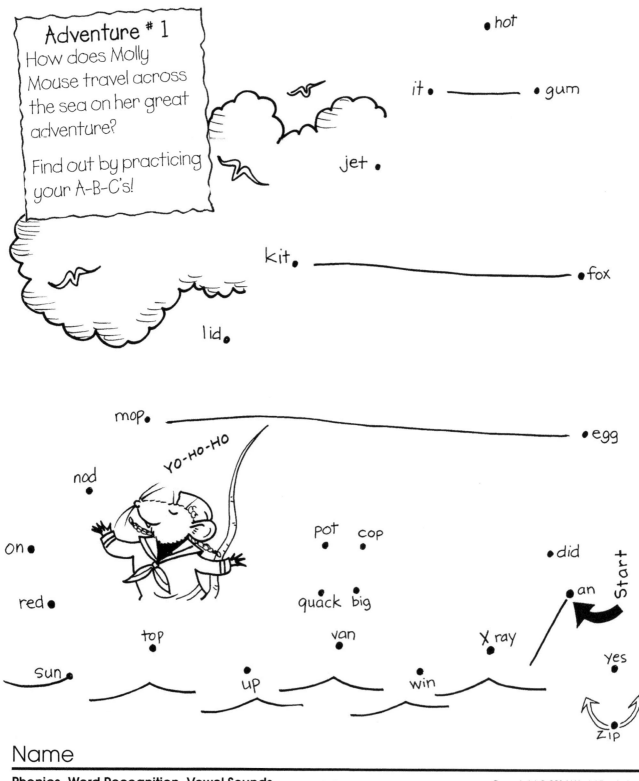

Adventure #1
How does Molly Mouse travel across the sea on her great adventure?

Find out by practicing your A-B-C's!

hot

it •———• gum

jet •

kit •———————• fox

lid •

mop •———————• egg

nod

YO-HO-HO

on •

red •

top

sun •

up

pot   cop

quack   big

van

win

X ray

did

an

Start

yes

Zip

Name

Clowning Around

Follow all the directions. Then circle all the words with **long vowel sounds**.

> ## Adventure # 2
> Did you ever think you would like to join a circus?
> Here's your chance to spend some time at the circus.
> Start off your visit by getting to know a clown.

1. Draw a bow in the clown's hair.

2. Draw a smile on her face.

3. Draw a kite in the air.

4. Draw a string from the kite to her hand.

5. Draw an ice cream cone in her other hand.

6. Color her nose red.

7. Color her cape green.

8. Draw a rose on each shoe.

9. Draw a cupcake in her pocket.

10. Draw a balloon for her pet.

Color the clown carefully.

Name

Phonics, Word Recognition, Vowel Sounds
Common Core Reinforcement Activities: 2nd Grade Language

Moose Tracking

Adventure # 3

Tracking the wild moose is quite a skill.
You can learn to follow moose in the north
woods of Canada and Alaska.
No shooting is allowed—except with a camera!

As you read about the moose, look for words with **double vowels**.

Write these words on the lines. Write each word only once. How many different words can you find?

I can't see anything!

The Adventure Company Jeep

There is a big, goofy-looking moose on the loose in the deep woods of northern Canada. Look! Can you see its trail of moose prints? What huge feet it has! The track of each foot is six inches (fifteen cm) long. It needs these large feet when it moves through cool pools and ponds looking for food. It likes to feed on plants and never eats toadstools or beetles. The moose is very quiet, so it is hard to find. This moose lives in Canada. Moose live in Alaska, too! But this moose would probably never live in a zoo. It would rather be free!

More tourists.

List the words that you found.

_____   _____   _____

_____   _____   _____

_____   _____   _____

_____   _____   _____

_____   _____   _____

_____   _____

There are _____ different words with double vowels.

Name _____

Rhino Watching

Read about the rhino and his bird friends.

Look for words with vowel combinations that give a **long e** sound. (This sound can be made by **e**, **ee**, **ie**, **ea**, or **y**.)

Circle the words that have a **long e** sound.

Adventure # 4

Come to Africa to watch the great rhinoceros. You'll find out that the rhino has some important friends.

The rhinoceros is an odd-looking beast that is said to be related to early dinosaurs. These days, there are not many rhinos left in Africa. Some hunters seek them out and kill them to take their large horns.

Their friends the egrets (pronounced ee-grets) come in flocks to sit on the backs of the rhinos and other large animals. The egrets sit on the animals' backs and wait for them to kick up insects with their feet. Then the egrets quickly fly down to eat up the insects. This is a good friendship, because the birds get a meal and the rhinos get rid of bothersome insects.

Name

A Helicopter Flight

Adventure # 5
Get on board our Adventure helicopter!
You'll have the most exciting ride.
We'll follow the crow through the clouds
to its lunch.
Everywhere it goes, we'll go, too!

Find the words with the sound made by **ow** in the word **crow**.

Color these clouds.

Draw a path for the crow to fly to each of these clouds.

down

clown

tow

town

low

crown

know

brown

plow

mow

how

cow

growl

show

grow

now

prowl

snow

flow

Name

Hurricane Watch

Solve each riddle with
a word that has something
to do with a storm.

Each word has a vowel
combination of **ea**, **ai**, **ou**, or **oa**.

Adventure # 6

Hurricane Matilda is storming in.
We can watch the storm, but not from
the boat.
We'll get to shore and find a safe place
for watching.

Riddle 1

Get me out of the water
When the wind starts to blow.
Row me right to the shore,
And don't be slow!

I am a _____.
(I rhyme with "float.")

Riddle 3

Don't play here today
With your shovel and pail!
You'll get swept out to sea
And get pounded with hail.

I am the _____.
(I rhyme with "peach.")

Riddle 2

We're crashing waves.
We toss ships around.
We wash over beaches
And cover the ground.

Our sound is _____.
(It rhymes with "crowd.")

Riddle 4

I pour from the skies
And drench the land.
I blow in your windows
And soak into the sand.

I am the _____.
(I rhyme with "pane.")

Name _____

Phonics, Word Recognition, Vowel Sounds
Common Core Reinforcement Activities: 2nd Grade Language

Reptile Races

Adventure # 7

Travel to the desert to watch a race between Tricky Lizard and Sticky-Tongued Snake. Which one will get the yummy first prize?

Tricky Lizard can only follow words with **long a** or **long e** sounds. Color its path to the prize **green**.

Sticky-Tongued Snake can only follow words with **long i**, **long o**, or **long u** sounds. Color its path **red**.

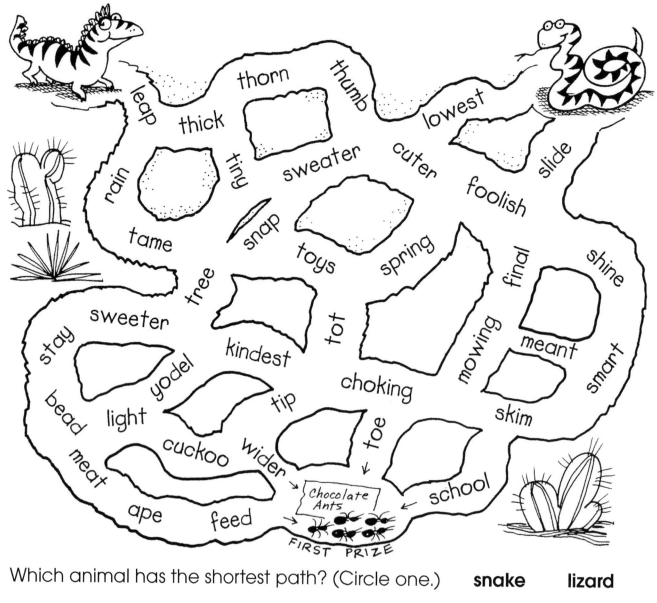

Which animal has the shortest path? (Circle one.)   **snake   lizard**

Name

Visit a Desert Hotel

Add a prefix or suffix to make a word that describes each animal. Choose from prefixes and suffixes on the suitcases below.

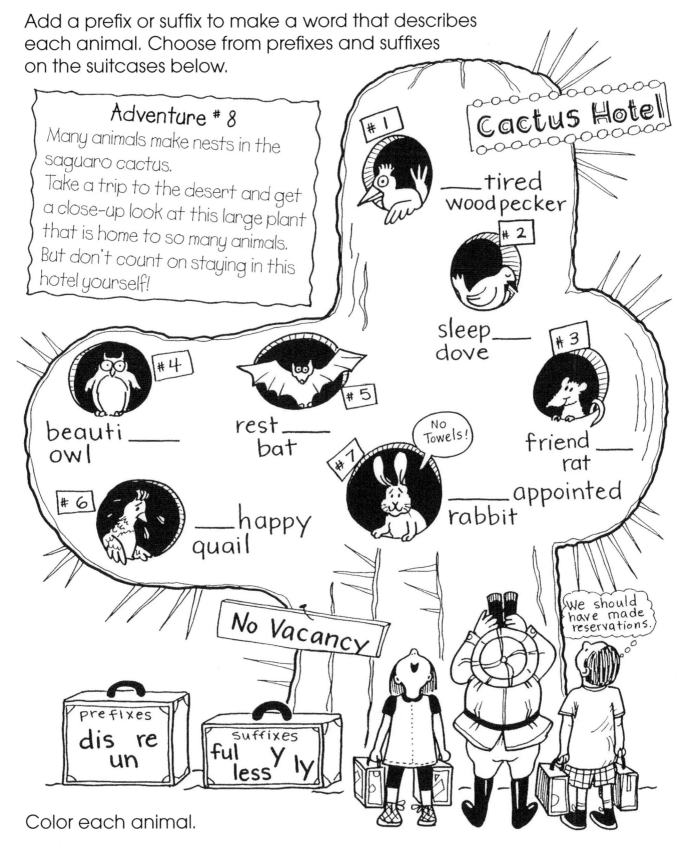

Adventure # 8

Many animals make nests in the saguaro cactus.
Take a trip to the desert and get a close-up look at this large plant that is home to so many animals.
But don't count on staying in this hotel yourself!

Cactus Hotel

#1 ___tired woodpecker

#2 sleep___ dove

#3 friend___ rat

#4 beauti___ owl

#5 rest___ bat

#6 ___happy quail

#7 ___appointed rabbit

No Towels!

No Vacancy

We should have made reservations.

prefixes
dis re un

suffixes
ful less y ly

Color each animal.

Name

Phonics, Word Recognition, Prefixes, Suffixes
Common Core Reinforcement Activities: 2nd Grade Language

Nighttime Detectives

A **root word** is a word that was there before prefixes or suffixes were added.

Look at the bold word in each of these sentences about nocturnal animals.

Decide what the root word is. Write it on the line.

Adventure # 9

In Australia, there are many animals that stay awake all night. These animals are called nocturnal. Sneak up and watch them carefully, because not all of them are friendly!

1. The platypus has a **supersize** bill.

   _____

2. Koala bears have **disappeared** from many areas.

   _____

3. The **poisonous** leaves of the eucalyptus tree do not harm koalas.

   _____

4. **Quietly** the desert shrew moves through the desert.

   _____

5. The Tasmanian devil is the **strangest** animal.

   _____

6. A marsupial mouse lemur sleeps **peacefully** all day.

   _____

7. Australia is home to some of the **largest** bats.

   _____

8. Stay around for daylight, and watch the **powerful** kangaroos jumping.

   _____

Shhh! It's a duck-billed platypus.

A platypus can eat 12,500 worms in a month.

Adventure Company Camp Site

Name _____

Rodeo Ride

Read the word at the top of each group.

Draw a lasso around the word that is the correct root word.

Remember: A **root word** is the word without any prefixes or suffixes added to it.

1. unstoppable

stop   able

unstop

stoppable

2. dangerous

danger

dan

dang

3. working

or

work

king

I'm as skillful with a lasso as a real cowgirl.

4. disagreeable

disagree

agreeable

agree   dis

This bronco is full of wildness !

5. blameless

am   less   blame

6. finest

fine   fin   nest

7. neighborhood

neigh   bor

neighbor

8. careful

full   are   care

I hope I don't mistakenly lasso myself !

9. untamed

un   tame

tamed   tam

10. unfriendliness

unfriendly   friendly

friendliness   friend

Name

Ski the Alps

Adventure # 11
The Alps have the best skiing in the world! Wax your skis and get ready for some beautiful sights!

The answers to the mountain puzzle are all homonyms.

Homonyms sound alike, but do not look alike.

One word in each clue sentence is the wrong homonym. Write the correct homonym into the puzzle.

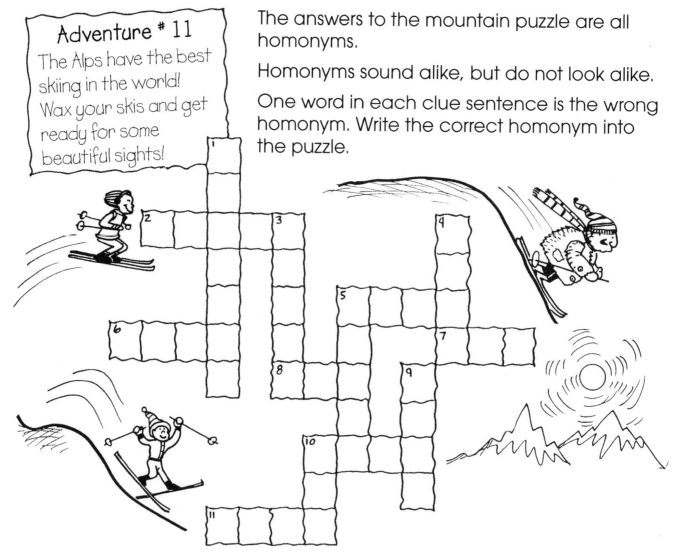

Down

1. The king rained for twenty years.
3. Good shoppers always look for sails.
4. The wind blue down a tree.
5. Let's take a ride in a plain.
9. "Please come hear."
10. This morning there was do on the grass.

Across

2. I have ten pears of socks.
5. She will pair the potatoes.
6. The storyteller told a tall tail.
7. Which weigh do we go?
8. She rowed her boat in the see.
10. I sent a letter to my deer aunt.
11. They new the truth.

Name

Through the Iceberg Maze

Adventure # 12

Bring warm clothes and be ready for a challenge.
We're heading across an icy ocean, and we have a lot of icebergs to dodge.

Draw a path across the water that passes between at least ten neighboring icebergs. Start by one of the top icebergs and end between the two on the bottom.

Read someone each word on the icebergs you pass.

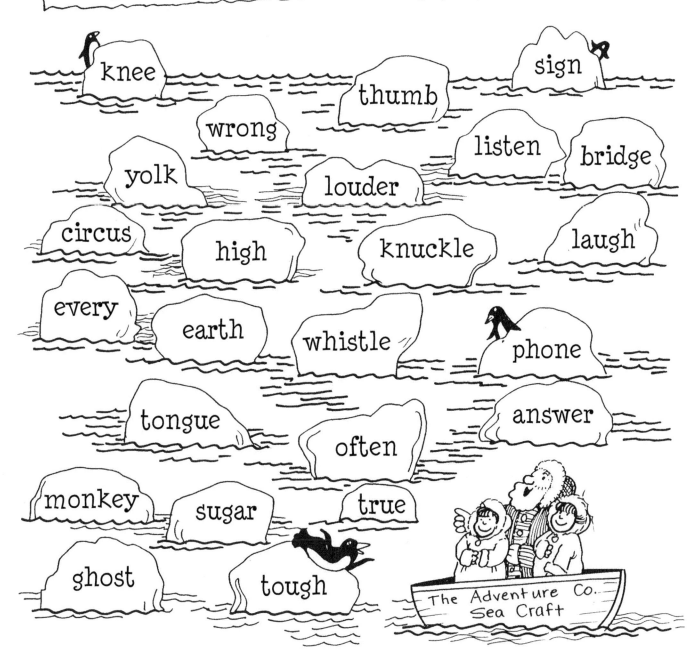

knee · sign · thumb · wrong · listen · bridge · yolk · louder · circus · high · knuckle · laugh · every · earth · whistle · phone · tongue · answer · often · monkey · sugar · true · ghost · tough

The Adventure Co. Sea Craft

Name

Phonics, Spelling-Sound Correspondence
Common Core Reinforcement Activities: 2nd Grade Language

A Thrilling Ride

The words on the Ferris wheel might sound differently than they are spelled

Show that you can read them. Choose the right one for each blank.

Adventure # 13
Ride the super duper Double-High Ferris Wheel at Adventureland! It will take you twice as high as any other Ferris wheel in the world.

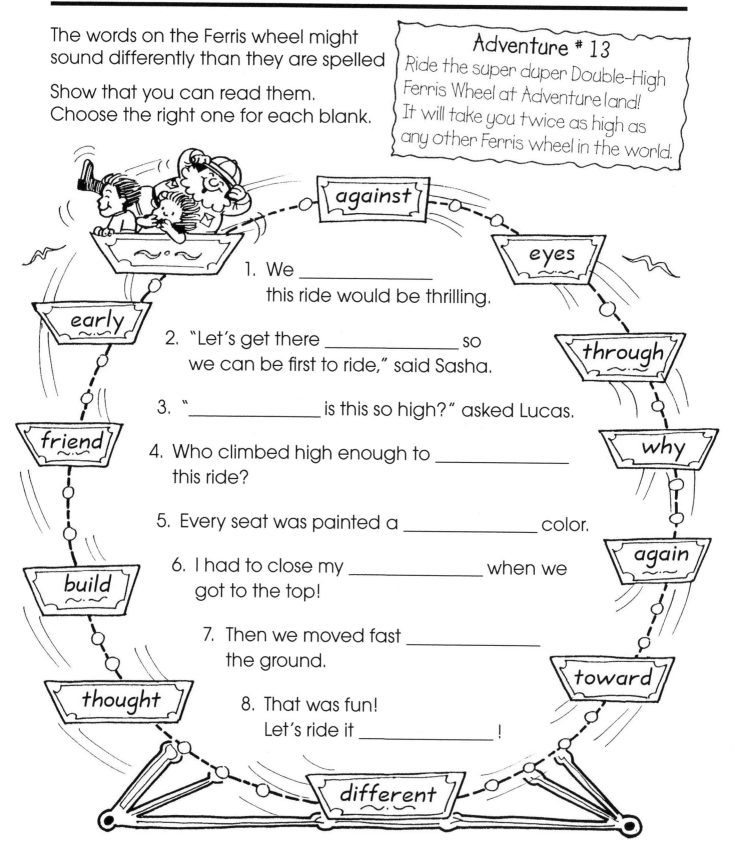

1. We _____ this ride would be thrilling.

2. "Let's get there _____ so we can be first to ride," said Sasha.

3. "_____ is this so high?" asked Lucas.

4. Who climbed high enough to _____ this ride?

5. Every seat was painted a _____ color.

6. I had to close my _____ when we got to the top!

7. Then we moved fast _____ the ground.

8. That was fun! Let's ride it _____ !

against

eyes

through

why

again

toward

different

thought

build

friend

early

Name _____

What's That Under the Sea?

Draw a line to connect the words
in alphabetical order.

Then you will see another sea creature.

What is it?

_____

Read each word out loud to a friend.

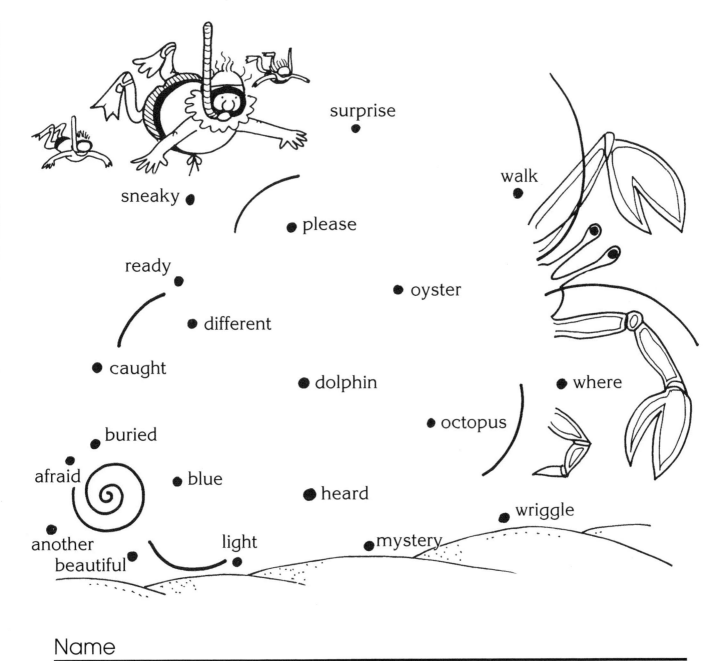

surprise

walk

sneaky

please

ready

oyster

different

caught

dolphin

where

octopus

buried

afraid

blue

heard

another

light

mystery

wriggle

beautiful

Name _____

Word Recognition, Irregularly Spelled Words
Common Core Reinforcement Activities: 2nd Grade Language

The Wild Boar Chase

1. Chase the wild boar through the maze of words.

2. Color only the spaces with words that are spelled correctly.

3. Then write the numbered letters on the lines at the bottom to find the name of some things in Borneo that are very large.

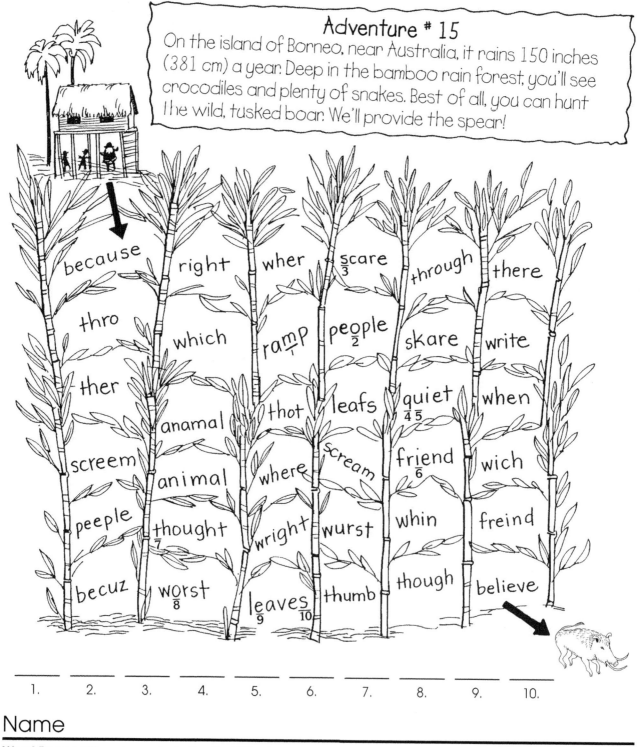

Adventure # 15

On the island of Borneo, near Australia, it rains 150 inches (381 cm) a year. Deep in the bamboo rain forest, you'll see crocodiles and plenty of snakes. Best of all, you can hunt the wild, tusked boar. We'll provide the spear!

because   right   wher   scare$_3$ through   there

thro   which   ramp$_1$ people$_2$ skare   write

ther   anamal   thot   leafs   quiet$_{45}$ when

screem   animal   where   scream   friend$_6$ wich

peeple   thought$_7$ wright   wurst   whin   freind

becuz   worst$_8$ leaves$_9$ thumb$_{10}$ though   believe

1. ___ 2. ___ 3. ___ 4. ___ 5. ___ 6. ___ 7. ___ 8. ___ 9. ___ 10. ___

Name _____

Deep in the Rain Forest

The rain forest is filled with unusual plants and lost vowels.

Write the missing vowels into the words in the picture.

Then write the first vowel from words 1, 3, 5, and 7 into the blanks in number 11.

You'll spell the name of a very long jungle animal.

1. r _ _ n
2. j _ ngl _
3. p _ rr _ t
4. b _ n _ _
5. m _ nk _ y
6. j _ g _ _ r
7. r _ ft
8. l _ _ f
9. v _ n _
10. r _ v _ r

I can grow to be 25 feet long!

11. _ n _ c _ nd _

Name

Word Recognition, Irregularly Spelled Words
Common Core Reinforcement Activities: 2nd Grade Language

A Twirling Ride

Adventure # 17
A real tornado is too dangerous to ride!
But you can ride the Tornado Slide at
Adventureland Fun Park! Try it out!

Read each word on the
Tornado Slide.

Choose 10 of the words.
Tell a friend what each
of them means.

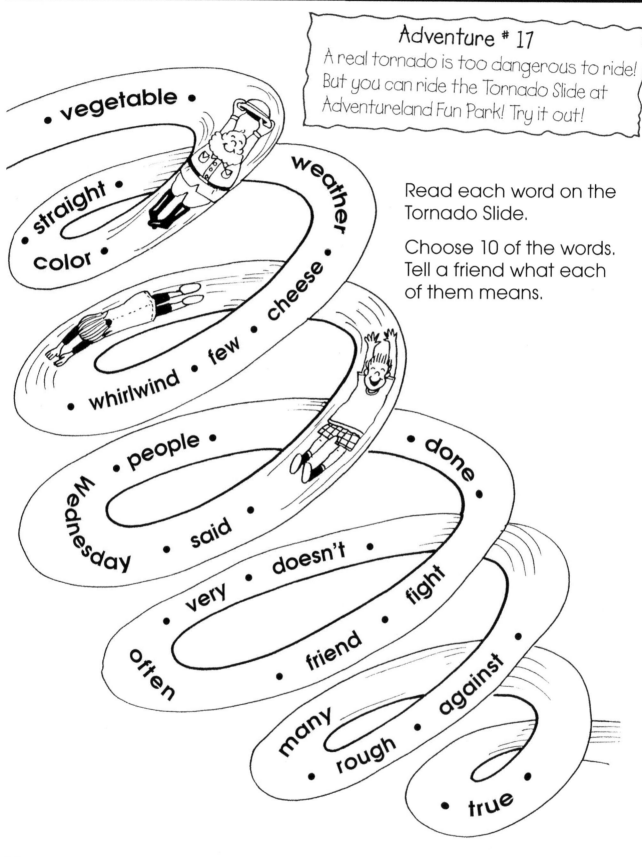

vegetable

straight

color

weather

cheese

few

whirlwind

people

Wednesday

said

done

very

doesn't

fight

often

friend

many

against

rough

true

Name

WRITING

Grade 2

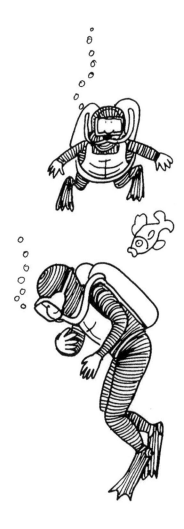

Choose Your Adventure

Read the signs that tell about some exciting adventures.

Choose an adventure that you would like to have.

Write about it on the next page (page 81).

Welcome to the Worldwide Adventure Company. We have thrilling adventures for everyone.

Sounds good.

Unusual Adventures!

Fight a fire-breathing dragon.

Ride a barrel over Niagara Falls.

Look inside meat-eating plants.

Steer a boat around icebergs.

Surf a huge wave.

Rocket through the solar system.

Follow a rare mountain gorilla.

Travel into the past.

Explore deep, dark caves.

Dangerous Adventures

SWAMP CRUISING

LION TAMING

ALLIGATOR WRESTLING

MOOSE TRACKING

HURRICANE CHASING

STALKING BIGFOOT

Use with page 81.

Name

Choose Your Adventure, continued

Read the list of adventures on the other page (page 80).
Write a sentence that tells what you will choose.

Write another sentence or two to tell why you want that adventure.

Write a good ending.

_____

_____

_____

_____

_____

_____

_____

_____

_____

_____

We're off to ride a camel!   Hold on tight!

blurp

POP POP

The Adventure Company

screech

_____

_____

_____

_____

Use with page 80.

Name

A Swamp Cruise

Do you think it is
a good idea to
wrestle an alligator?

Give your opinion.

Give reasons for
your opinion.

Write an ending.

_____

_____

_____

_____

_____

_____

_____

_____

_____

_____

Name

Over the Edge

These people have decided to ride a barrel over a waterfall.

Do you think this would be too dangerous? Give your opinion.

Give reasons for your opinion.

Write an ending.

_____

_____

_____

_____

_____

_____

_____

_____

_____

_____

_____

_____

_____

_____

_____

Name

Text Types: Opinion
Common Core Reinforcement Activities: 2nd Grade Language

Meet the Meat Eaters

Meat-eating plants give off sweet-smelling, sticky nectar.

Adventure # 20
Visit meat-eating plants around the world!
But keep your fingers in your pockets!

The smell attracts insects. The insects get stuck and can't get away. Then the plant snaps shut and traps them.

Tell the fly to keep away from this plant. Tell him why.

Write a beginning. Write reasons. Write an ending.

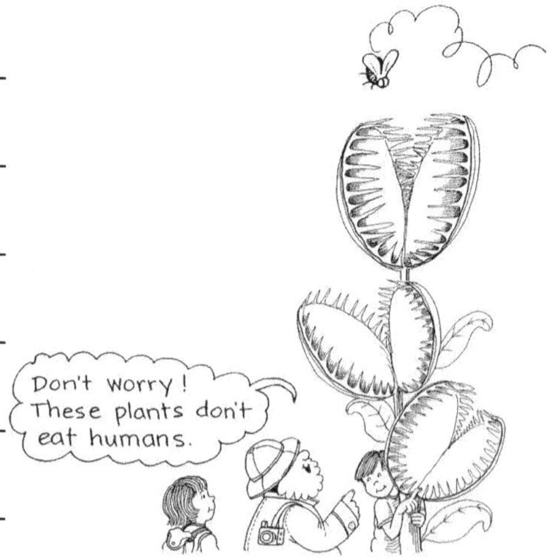
Don't worry! These plants don't eat humans.

Name

Hunt for Pirate Treasure

Adventure # 21

Bring a shovel and a sack for treasure. We'll provide the map! Take a trip to the deserted Island of the Bones and dig for pirate's treasure.

How can someone find a buried treasure?

What should they do when they find it?

Explain how to hunt for pirate treasure.

Tell what to do when it is found.

Write a good ending.

Name

Text Types: Informative/Explanatory
Common Core Reinforcement Activities: 2nd Grade Language

Fire Danger!

How can you fight a dragon?

You decide.

Write some rules for fighting a fire-breathing dragon.

Number the rules.

Rules for Fighting a Dragon

Name

Search for Bigfoot

Adventure # 23

Some people look for a big hairy creature with huge feet. Join a search for Bigfoot. Walk in silence. Listen for the sound of big feet walking.

Write a beginning for a story about these Bigfoot trackers.

Then tell what happens.

Write a good ending.

_____

_____

_____

_____

_____

_____

_____

_____

_____

_____

_____

_____

come along!

Name

Text Types: Narrative
Common Core Reinforcement Activities: 2nd Grade Language

Underwater Surprises

Adventure # 24

First we'll teach you how to scuba dive.
Then you can come with us to enjoy the undersea world.
Bring your waterproof camera!

What are the divers thinking about their underwater visit?

Write a thought that you imagine for each diver.
Write complete sentences.
Use some of the words on the shells.

Diver #1 thought: _____

_____

_____

Diver #2 thought: _____

_____

_____

Diver #3 thought: _____

_____

_____

remember deep friendly adventure surprise sink colorful wonder amazed sights

Name _____

Go Spelunking!

These friends are exploring a cave together.

What would you like to know about their adventure? Write five questions to ask them.

Use the picture to help you think about questions.

1. _____

_____

2. _____

_____

3. _____

_____

4. _____

_____

5. _____

_____

Name

A Bumpy Camel Ride

It is a great treat to ride a camel.

Invite someone to join you on this adventure. Write an invitation!

Use your own ideas and your own words.

Adventure # 26

Ride a furry Bactrian camel through the grasslands of Asia. Bring your camera and be prepared for a bumpy, lumpy ride!

You are invited to take a _____ camel ride.

Bring along these things: _____

_____

_____

_____

You can expect to see _____

_____

_____

_____

The ride will be bumpy because _____

_____

_____

_____

Giddy-up

The trip starts at _____

_____

Be here on time!

Name _____

A Low-Down Place

Finish the poems about this low, low place.

Use your imagination and your own words.

Adventure # 27

You bring the camera!
We'll bring the submarine!
You can explore the
lowest spot on Earth!

The lowest spot ever reached is the Marianas Trench in the Pacific Ocean. It is 36,000 feet below sea level!

The Adventure Co. Submarine

1. The trench is deep.

   Our trip is slow.

   I wonder if

   _____

2. Watch out for sharks!

   Enjoy the view!

   I see ten fish

   _____ ?

3. As we get down low

   Everything gets dark.

   I hope the submarine knows

   _____ !

4. Many creatures

   Live deep in the sea.

   I'm curious about them.

   Are they _____ ?

Name

Develop and Revise Writing
Common Core Reinforcement Activities: 2nd Grade Language

A Lot of Hot Air

Adventure # 28
Rise high above the Earth
in a hot air-balloon.
Float along and see
wonderful sights!
Watch out for birds!

Flying in a hot-air balloon is lots of fun!

It is also fun to tell about the ride.

Finish the sentences.

1. This balloon is going as high as _____

_____ .

2. The ride is more thrilling than _____

_____ .

3. The wind today is as gentle as _____

_____ .

4. The people down below look as _____ as

_____ .

5. J.J. is so excited! He squeals like a _____

_____ .

6. I would rather ride in a balloon than _____

_____ .

Name

Time Travel

Did you know that the word *dinosaur* means "terrifying lizard"?

T. rex was the largest meat-eating dinosaur of all!
This adventure will take you back in time to meet one.

But what will you learn?

Find a book about dinosaurs.
Write 5 things it tells you about *Tyrannosaurus rex*.

Five Things I Learned About *T. rex*

1. _____

_____

2. _____

_____

3. _____

_____

4. _____

_____

5. _____

_____

Name

Alaska Campout

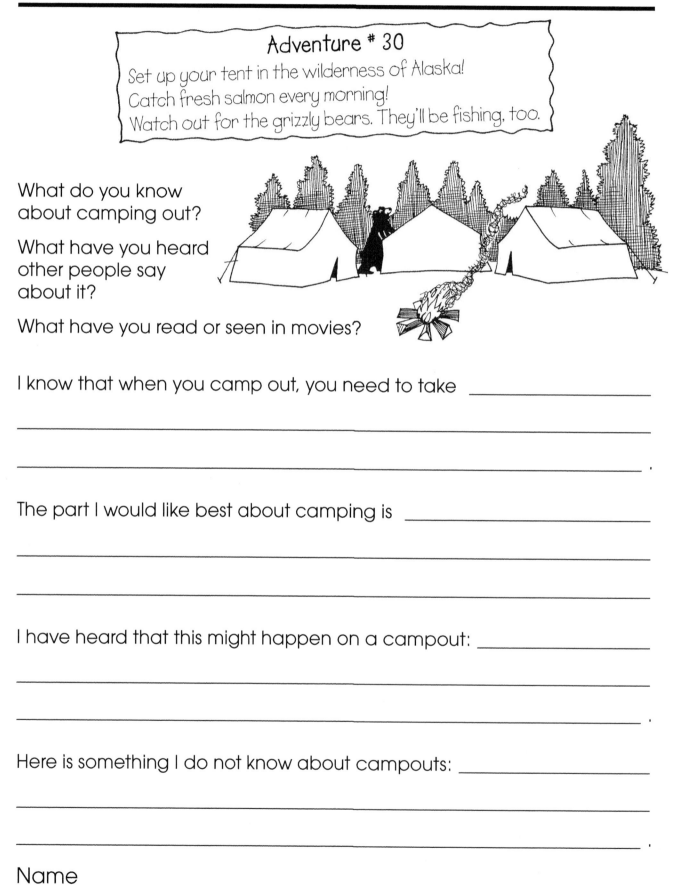

Adventure # 30

Set up your tent in the wilderness of Alaska!
Catch fresh salmon every morning!
Watch out for the grizzly bears. They'll be fishing, too.

What do you know about camping out?

What have you heard other people say about it?

What have you read or seen in movies?

I know that when you camp out, you need to take _____

_____

_____ .

The part I would like best about camping is _____

_____

_____ .

I have heard that this might happen on a campout: _____

_____

_____ .

Here is something I do not know about campouts: _____

_____

_____ .

Name

LANGUAGE

Grade 2

Milton the Magnificent

What will Milton pull out of his hat?

Circle the first noun in each sentence.

A noun names a person, place, or thing.

Write the first letter of that noun in the matching blank below.

Then draw the surprise in Milton's hand.

Abracadabra!

1. She plays in a bundle of blankets.

2. She never needs an umbrella.

3. She does not go to school.

4. She plays with a herd of friends.

5. She's afraid of yaks.

6. She loves to sleep in the kitchen.

7. She is not an iguana.

8. She visits Milton's troop of clowns.

9. She has a sticky, pink tongue.

10. She does not like eggs.

11. Her curious nose sniffs everything!

___ ___ ___ ___ ___ ___ ___ ___ ___ ___ ___
 1   2   3   4   5   6   7   8   9   10 11

Name

Step Right Up!

A plural noun names more than one of something.

"Step right up!" "Win great prizes!" "It's so easy!"

Listen to the shouts along the carnival arcade. Look at all the prizes to win.

Clyde Clown would like to win more than one!

Write the plural form of each noun in the box under the picture.

mouse

bunny

bear

knife

camera

butterfly

puppy

turtle

fish

glass

radio

monkey

duck

pennant

hippo

Name

Conventions: Plural Nouns
Common Core Reinforcement Activities: 2nd Grade Language

Monkey Action

What is more fun than a barrel of monkeys? Not much!

This barrel holds a puzzle about the actions of monkeys.

Every word in the puzzle is the **past form** of a verb.

Use the clues on the next page (page 99) to help you write the answers for the puzzle.

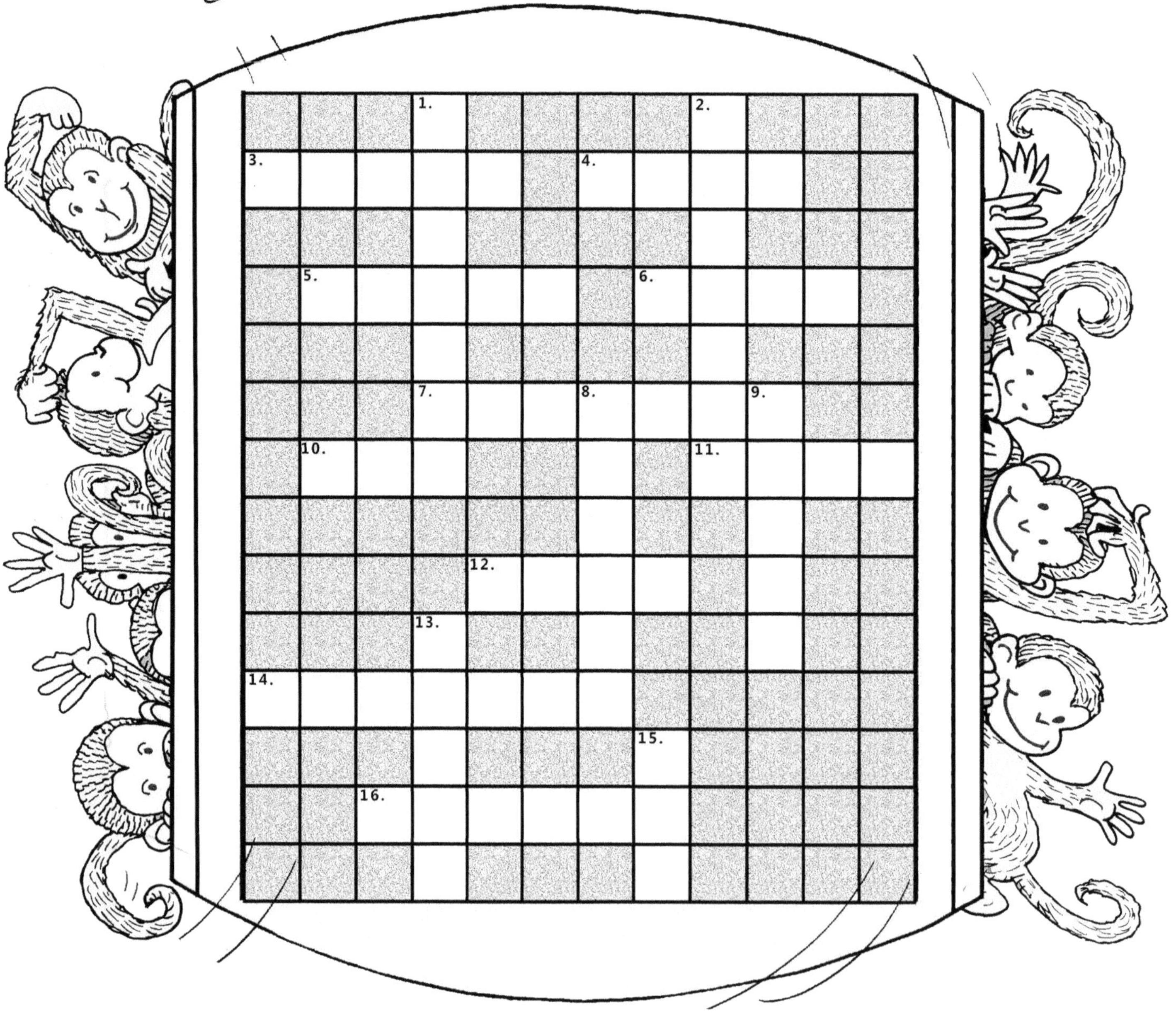

Use with page 99.

Name _____

Monkey Action, continued

Use these clues to finish the puzzle on page 98.

Circle the first verb in each sentence.

Write its past form into the puzzle.

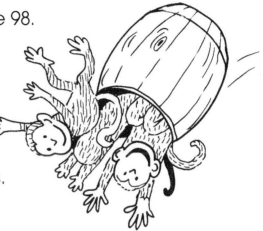

Down

1. We bring out a barrel for the monkeys.

2. The monkeys enjoy it!

8. Gonzo raises his head over the edge.

9. Millie, dry the tears from your eyes!

13. Millie cries tears of laughter.

15. Monkeys meet each other at the top of the barrel.

Across

3. We hear so much noise from these monkeys!

4. Arnie, you go first!

5. Hattie, find Lucy at the bottom!

6. Mel might lose her rings while she jumps.

7. George, hurry back to the barrel.

10. Oh, no! Lucas accidentally bites his lip!

11. They draw straws to see who would be first.

12. Candy, rise up fast!

14. Sammy worries that he might get hurt.

16. Finally, the monkeys become tired.

Name

Conventions: Past Tense Verbs
Common Core Reinforcement Activities: 2nd Grade Language

Take a Spin

The Clown-Around Kids had great fun on the spinning teacups. When they finished, they were dizzy.

Read about the pronouns that include the word "self."

Read the sentence on each teacup.

If the sentence uses a reflexive pronoun, color the cup and saucer.

A reflexive pronoun contains the word "self" when it refers to some person, persons, or things.

These are reflexive pronouns: myself, yourself, himself, herself, itself, ourselves, yourselves, themselves.

1. Does the teacup spin by itself?

2. Boppo and Lulu giggle at themselves.

3. Can you make yours go faster?

4. Georgie rode by himself.

5. Maizie rode until she was sick.

6. "I'm spinning by myself!" cried Mel.

Name _____

The Champion

An **adjective** describes a noun. It can tell color, size, shape, number, or what kind.

Tonight is the big night.

Zelda is the skeeball champion of the whole carnival!

She is undefeated for the entire year.

She needs 100 points to keep her lead.

An **adverb** describes a verb. It tells how, when, where, or how often something happened.

Use green to circle all the adjectives that describe the bold nouns. Zelda gets 10 points for each adjective.

Use red to circle all the adverbs that describe the bold verbs. Zelda gets 5 points for each adverb.

Write the points for each sentence.

_____ 1. Zelda wore her lucky purple **hat** to the big **game**.

_____ 2. Six good **friends cheered** loudly for Zelda.

_____ 3. She chose new, striped **balls** for this important **game**.

_____ 4. The first **ball rolled** smoothly down in a straight **path**.

_____ 5. Four noisy teenage **clowns** used the lane next to hers.

_____ 6. The second **ball** easily **got** the highest **score**.

_____ 7. She **stopped** suddenly for a treat of pink cotton **candy**.

_____ 8. When the long **night** was over, did she have a winning **score**?

Name

Conventions: Adjectives and Adverbs
Common Core Reinforcement Activities: 2nd Grade Language

Adventures on the High Wire

Amazing! Henrietta can walk on a skinny wire high off the ground!

It is a long, long way down if she falls.

Will she stay on the wire? Find out!

An adverb describes a verb. It tells **how, when, where,** or **how often** something happened.

As you read, circle the adverb in each sentence that tells **how, when, where**, or **how often** about the verb. The clue at the end of each sentence will help you.

1. Henrietta climbed slowly up the ladder to the wire. .. (**Climbed** how?)

2. She knew that she would start her act soon. ....(**Would start** when?)

3. She did not look down at the crowd. ....(**Did not look** where?)

4. Carefully, she stepped onto the wire. .... (**Stepped** how?)

5. She looked only ahead. ....(**Looked** where?)

6. She held on tightly to her umbrella. .... (**Held** how?)

7. She never felt nervous at the beginning. ....(**Felt** how often?)

8. She frequently felt nervous halfway across. ....(**Felt** how often?)

9. She began to breathe deeply to relax. ....(**Breathed** how?)

10. Soon she would reach the other side. ....(**Would reach** when?)

11. Suddenly she sneezed. .... (**Sneezed** how?)

12. She fell rapidly toward the ground. .... (**Fell** how?)

13. She landed safely in the net. ....(**Landed** how?)

14. "Tomorrow I will stay on the wire!" she said. ....(**Will stay** when?)

Name _____

Leaping Through Fire

A complete sentence has a naming part and an action part.

It's so much fun to watch this act!

Waldo has trained his dogs to leap through burning hoops. The dogs don't even act afraid (except for one).

Finish each sentence fragment to make it a complete sentence.

1. through the ring of fire.

2. Rover can

3. is almost there.

4. wants to go first.

5. is afraid.

6. The fire

7. looks dangerous.

8. His floppy ears

Lucky — I can't do it!

Trixie

Spot

Rover

Copyright © 2014 World Book, Inc./
Incentive Publications, Chicago, IL

Conventions: Sentences
Common Core Reinforcement Activities: 2nd Grade Language

A Bunch of Balloons

The balloons on the sentences are unfinished!

Make each one into a complete sentence.
Some of them can be questions or exclamations.

Color the balloons:
   Blue = statements
   Red = questions
   Yellow = exclamations

1. That dog can

2. Is that clown

3. Don't pop

4. Do these cost

5. Look out for

6. Her costume is

7. Oh, no! Don't

8. How many

9. ____ is so silly

10. Where did she get

Name

Unusual Talents

Ellie, the elephant, might have some unusual talents.

It is possible she can do the things her friends say she can, but we can't be sure!

Change each statement about Ellie into a question to show that you wonder if she really does have these talents!

A question asks something. It ends with a ?

Ellie walks on the high wire.

Does Ellie walk on the high wire ?

Can I believe my eyes ?

oh, oh, oh

Write each statement as a question.

1. That is Ellie on the high wire. _____

2. It is true that the elephant can fly. _____

3. Ellie can juggle pies. _____

4. Ellie does know how to ride a unicycle. _____

5. The elephant was jumping through a ring of fire. _____

6. Ellie has eaten all the cotton candy. _____

Name _____

Conventions: Sentences
Common Core Reinforcement Activities: 2nd Grade Language

Ups and Downs

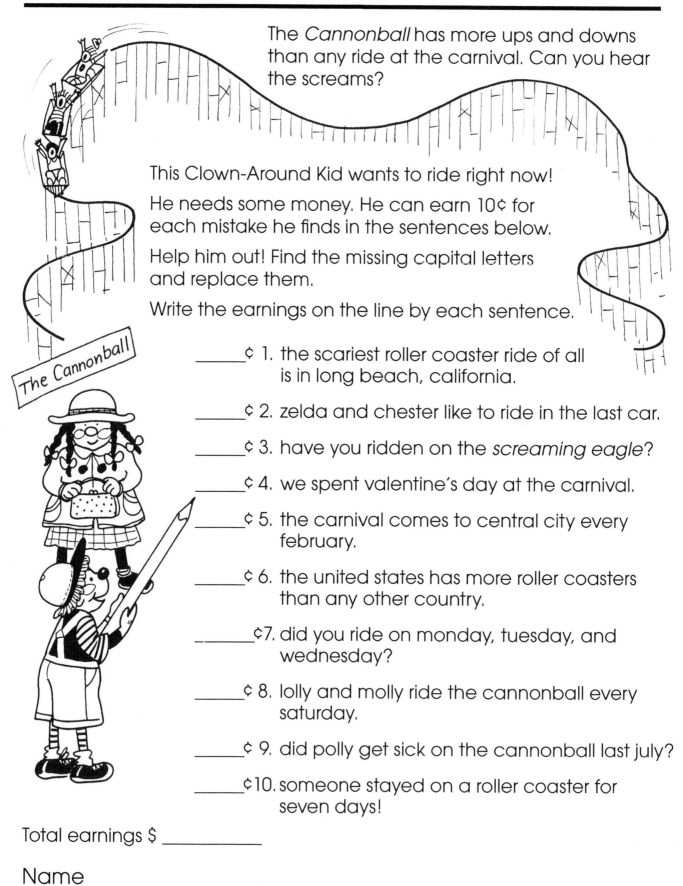

The *Cannonball* has more ups and downs than any ride at the carnival. Can you hear the screams?

This Clown-Around Kid wants to ride right now!

He needs some money. He can earn 10¢ for each mistake he finds in the sentences below.

Help him out! Find the missing capital letters and replace them.

Write the earnings on the line by each sentence.

_____¢ 1. the scariest roller coaster ride of all is in long beach, california.

_____¢ 2. zelda and chester like to ride in the last car.

_____¢ 3. have you ridden on the *screaming eagle*?

_____¢ 4. we spent valentine's day at the carnival.

_____¢ 5. the carnival comes to central city every february.

_____¢ 6. the united states has more roller coasters than any other country.

_____¢ 7. did you ride on monday, tuesday, and wednesday?

_____¢ 8. lolly and molly ride the cannonball every saturday.

_____¢ 9. did polly get sick on the cannonball last july?

_____¢ 10. someone stayed on a roller coaster for seven days!

The Cannonball

Total earnings $ _____

Name _____

Letters from the Circus

Sammy Seal and Ella Elephant wrote letters to their friend Bella. They told her about some of the exciting events of the circus.

They forgot the commas! Write commas where they are needed.

Use commas in the greeting and closing, the date, and the address.

55 Circus Lane
Clowntown Iowa

June 10 2013

Dear Bella
Today Tina's pet snake got loose during the circus. It scared the wrinkled elephants. They knocked over the lion tamer. All the monkeys ran into the audience. It was so funny.

Your friend
Sammy

55 Circus Lane
Clowntown Iowa

June 11 2013

Dear Bella
What fun the circus was today! Fred the fire-eater swallowed a can of fried worms. We held our breath when Suzu tumbled off the high wire. It's a good thing that the four dancing bears caught her.

Your friend
Ella

Name _____

Conventions: Punctuation—Commas
Common Core Reinforcement Activities: 2nd Grade Language

On the Merry-Go-Round

It is hard to resist a ride on a good merry-go-round!

This one is a favorite spot for the Clown-Around Kids.

The merry-go-round could use some decoration!

Follow the directions to give it some color!

Add the missing apostrophes. After you fix each sentence, color the part of the ride that is named next to that sentence.

Color

poles	1. The clown kids cant wait to ride the merry-go-round!
floor	2. Dont you wish you could ride too?
elephant	3. Only one horses tail is curly.
giraffe	4. The giraffes rider is the youngest clown kid.
unicorn	5. Shouldnt Zippo be holding on to the pole?
zebra	6. Charlie wont fall off the unicorn.
roof	7. Look at the elephants fancy hat!
clowns	8. The kids love the merry-go-rounds music.

Name

Weird, Wacky Mirrors

Snuffles has wandered into the Hall of Wacky Mirrors.
These mirrors make some things look strange!

In each mirror, circle the word that is spelled wrong.

Write it correctly at the bottom of the mirror.

1.
needle
bugle
poodel

2.
wishes
dishs
bushes

3.
driped
sagged
popped

4.
couff
laugh
trough

5.
monkeys
vallies
donkeys

6.
tomorow
borrow
sorrow

7.
bosses
glases
kisses

8.
could
should
wuld

9.
solos
pianoes
cellos

10.
thum
numb
comb

11.
cities
babys
ladies

12.
elfs
knives
leaves

Name

Conventions: Spelling
Common Core Reinforcement Activities: 2nd Grade Language

Sniffing Out Mistakes

It is Sniffy's job to track down misspelled words around the carnival grounds.

He catches the words and pushes them into the trash can with his broom. Help him with his job by drawing a path for him to sweep.

Draw a path that connects all the misspelled words.

Write each wrong word correctly.

choice

sed   duz   gon

meny   double   they   ar   answer

brought   laff   brot

thay   gone

helpful   beautaful

weather   where

many

beautiful   pepel   buy

suprize   once   helpful

helpful   friend

people   anser   wher

believe   choise   dubble

wether   does   wunce

laugh   surprise

trash

Fun on the Circus Train

The clowns on the circus train are having a good time on their ride.

Read their speech bubbles!

Here are some other things they said and did. Some words are not spelled correctly. Use your dictionary to find the bold words. Write them correctly on the blank lines.

_____ 1. "Will we **desend** any hills?" asked Bubbles.

_____ 2. The **enginere** shouted, "Are you ready?"

_____ 3. Is it true that the ride will last **twelv** minutes?" asked Mrs. Clown.

_____ 4. The twins squealed and **claped** their hands.

_____ 5. "Hold on, **evrybuddy**!" hollered Danno.

_____ 6. The little clown said, "The ride was faster **yesturday**."

Name

Conventions: Spelling
Common Core Reinforcement Activities: 2nd Grade Language

Ring-Toss Talk

The ring toss is a favorite game for Zeke and Zelda Clown.

They try to get rings around the bottles. Help them out!

Which conversations show good language use for school?

Color the pins with the numbers of those sentences.

Add up the numbers to find their score.

1. "Step right up."
   "Try the ring toss!"

2. "Zeke, you did not miss once!"
   "What a great job, Zeke!"

3. "Zelda, you got three in a row!"
   "I am so proud."

4. "How'd ya do that Zelda?"
   "I dunno."

5. "Wanna try again Zeke?"
   "Nope, you go again."

6. "Zelda, how did you learn that?"
   "I practiced for a year."

7. "I wanna play like you."
   "Not a chance!"

8. "You knocked down four pins!"
   "Yes, I won a stuffed giraffe."

9. "My best prize was a TV."
   "Wow, that is a great prize!"

10. "Don't ya do nothing else?"
    "Naw, not much."

Name

Mystery on the Train

Read about the mysterious train trip. Notice the words in bold print.

A train raced along the tracks on a snowy night. The **forecast** called for many feet of snow. One passenger, Frannie Frog, felt that something strange would happen.

Frannie saw a cat covered in a **lumpy** coat. He moved slowly. He kept his hands **shoved** deep in his pockets. He looked over his shoulder **frequently**.

The train stopped with a **screech**. Everything went black. When the lights came on, many passengers screamed that their purses or computers were missing. The mysterious cat was **absent** from the train.

Tell what you think each of these words means.

1. forecast _____

2. shoved _____

3. screech _____

4. lumpy _____

5. frequently _____

6. absent _____

Name

Vocabulary: Word Meaning, Context
Common Core Reinforcement Activities: 2nd Grade Language

The Great Taco Mystery

A hundred tacos are missing from Cousin Pepito's Taco Stand. They were stolen before 9:00 this morning. Boot prints were found in the sand outside the stand.

Read the clues that Pepito found.
Tell the meaning of each word in bold type.

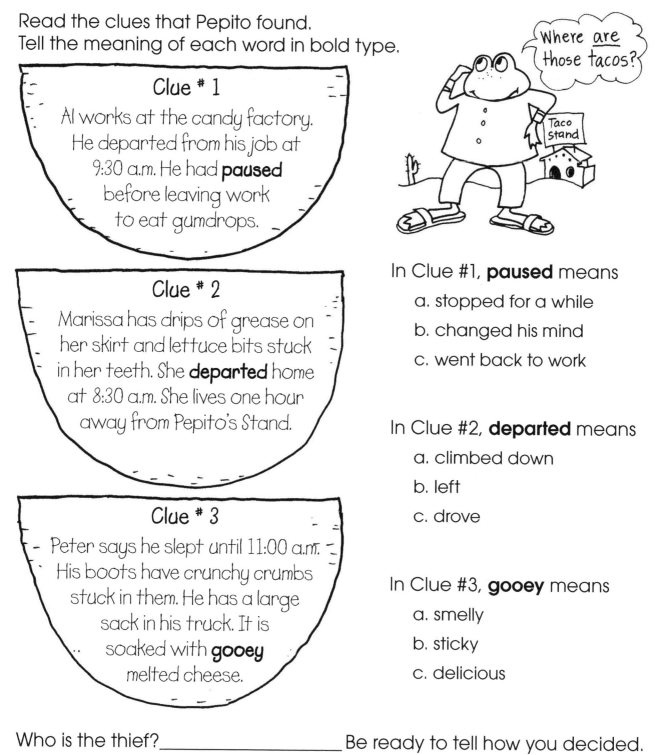

Where are those tacos?

Taco Stand

Clue # 1

Al works at the candy factory. He departed from his job at 9:30 a.m. He had **paused** before leaving work to eat gumdrops.

Clue # 2

Marissa has drips of grease on her skirt and lettuce bits stuck in her teeth. She **departed** home at 8:30 a.m. She lives one hour away from Pepito's Stand.

Clue # 3

Peter says he slept until 11:00 a.m. His boots have crunchy crumbs stuck in them. He has a large sack in his truck. It is soaked with **gooey** melted cheese.

In Clue #1, **paused** means
    a. stopped for a while
    b. changed his mind
    c. went back to work

In Clue #2, **departed** means
    a. climbed down
    b. left
    c. drove

In Clue #3, **gooey** means
    a. smelly
    b. sticky
    c. delicious

Who is the thief?_____ Be ready to tell how you decided.

Name

Safety on the Slopes

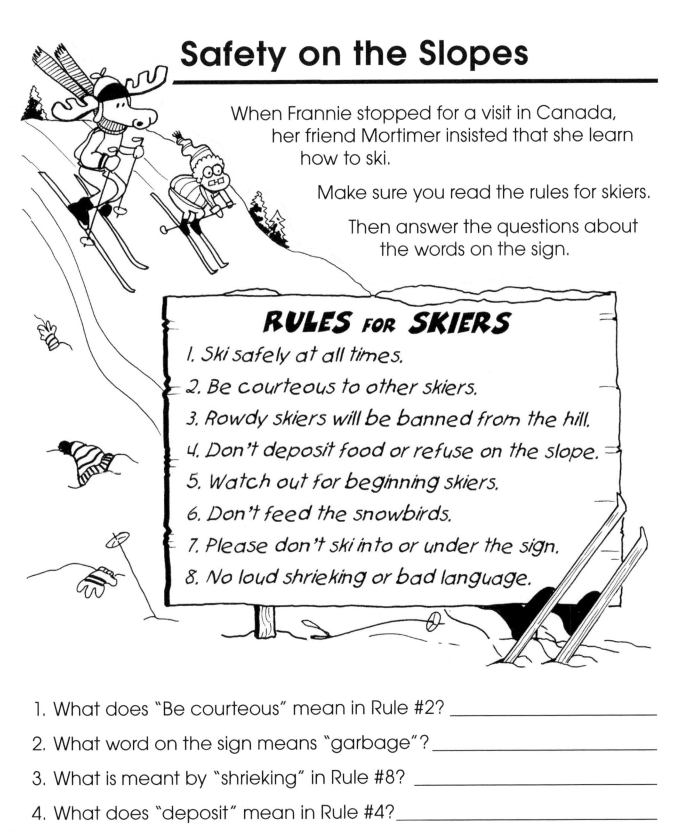

When Frannie stopped for a visit in Canada, her friend Mortimer insisted that she learn how to ski.

Make sure you read the rules for skiers.

Then answer the questions about the words on the sign.

RULES FOR SKIERS

1. Ski safely at all times.
2. Be courteous to other skiers.
3. Rowdy skiers will be banned from the hill.
4. Don't deposit food or refuse on the slope.
5. Watch out for beginning skiers.
6. Don't feed the snowbirds.
7. Please don't ski into or under the sign.
8. No loud shrieking or bad language.

1. What does "Be courteous" mean in Rule #2? _____

2. What word on the sign means "garbage"? _____

3. What is meant by "shrieking" in Rule #8? _____

4. What does "deposit" mean in Rule #4? _____

5. What word on the sign means "hill"? _____

6. What is meant by "Rowdy skiers will be banned" in Rule #3? _____

_____

Name

Vocabulary: Word Meaning, Prefixes
Common Core Reinforcement Activities: 2nd Grade Language

Track the Mountain Gorilla

Look at the bold word
in each sentence.

Finish writing its definition.

1. A mountain gorilla is a member of an **endangered** species.

   Endangered means *to cause to be in* _____

   _____ .

2. Many of the gorillas have **disappeared**.

   Disappeared means *the opposite of* _____

   _____ .

3. It is hard to see these gorillas. It's almost **impossible**.

   Impossible means _____

   _____ .

4. Hunters have **removed** too many gorillas.

   Removed means _____

   _____ .

5. If the gorillas are **unprotected**, they will be in danger.

   Unprotected means _____

   _____ .

6. Humans must **cooperate** to save the gorillas.

   Cooperate means *operate (or work)* _____

   _____ .

Name _____

Vocabulary: Word Meaning, Suffixes
Common Core Reinforcement Activities: 2nd Grade Language

Twice as Nice

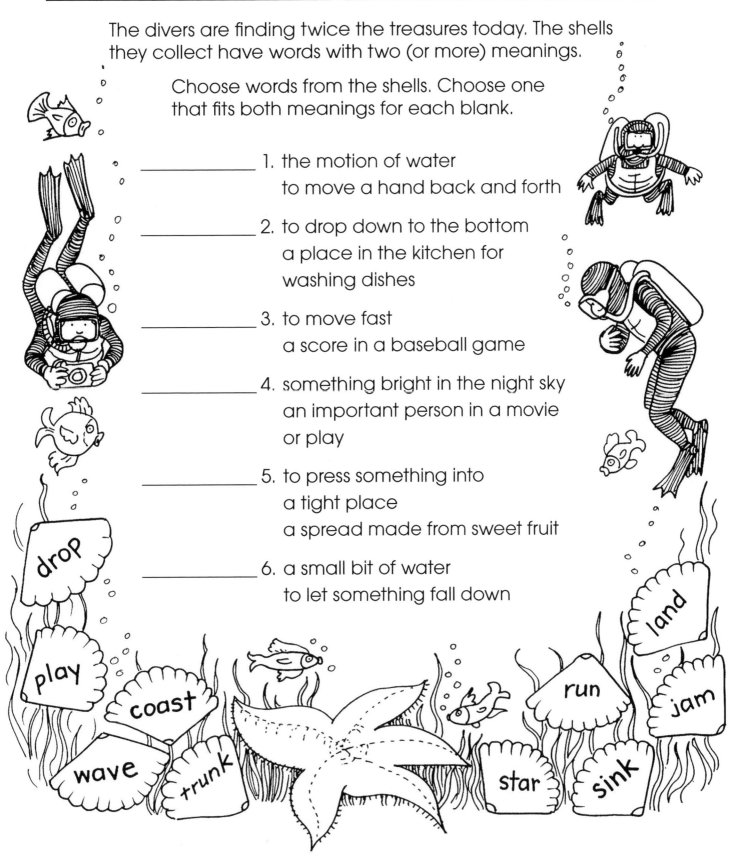

The divers are finding twice the treasures today. The shells they collect have words with two (or more) meanings.

Choose words from the shells. Choose one that fits both meanings for each blank.

_____ 1. the motion of water
to move a hand back and forth

_____ 2. to drop down to the bottom
a place in the kitchen for washing dishes

_____ 3. to move fast
a score in a baseball game

_____ 4. something bright in the night sky
an important person in a movie or play

_____ 5. to press something into a tight place
a spread made from sweet fruit

_____ 6. a small bit of water
to let something fall down

drop

play

coast

wave

trunk

land

jam

run

star

sink

Name _____

Vocabulary: Multiple Meanings
Common Core Reinforcement Activities: 2nd Grade Language

Double the Fun

The McFrog twins have double the ice cream they usually get.

Their cones are full of double-good words, too!

Each word has a root you probably know.

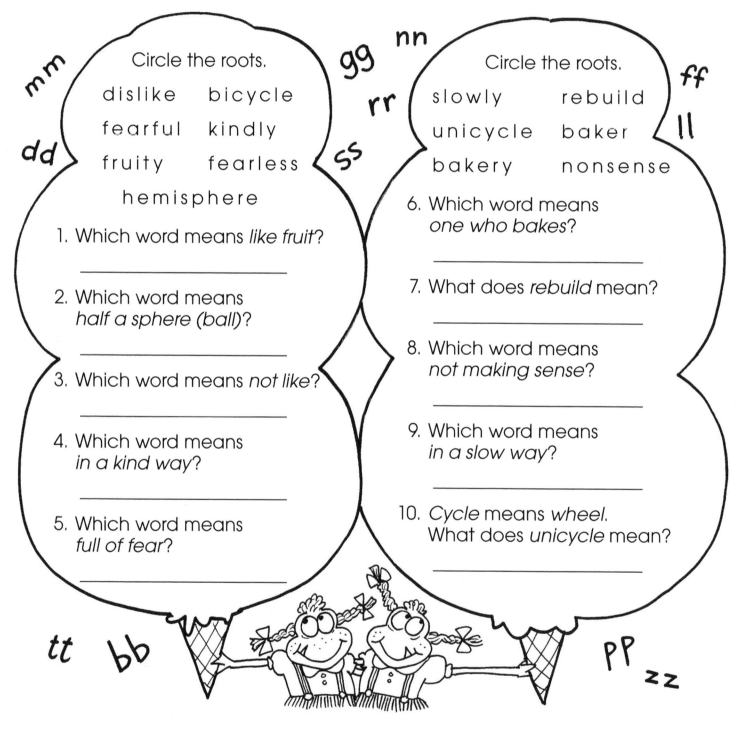

mm
dd
gg
nn
rr
ss

Circle the roots.

dislike   bicycle

fearful   kindly

fruity   fearless

hemisphere

1. Which word means *like fruit*?

   _____

2. Which word means
   half a sphere (ball)?

   _____

3. Which word means *not like*?

   _____

4. Which word means
   in a kind way?

   _____

5. Which word means
   full of fear?

   _____

ff
ll

Circle the roots.

slowly   rebuild

unicycle   baker

bakery   nonsense

6. Which word means
   one who bakes?

   _____

7. What does *rebuild* mean?

   _____

8. Which word means
   not making sense?

   _____

9. Which word means
   in a slow way?

   _____

10. *Cycle* means *wheel*.
    What does *unicycle* mean?

   _____

tt   bb   PP   zz

Name _____

Two Words Make New Words

The words in Oscar's pond have special talent. They can each join with another word to make a compound word.

The compound word will have a new meaning.

Water is the special *liquid* in the pond. Fall means *to tumble down.* A waterfall is *liquid that tumbles down.*

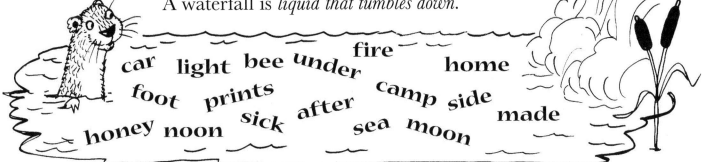

car light bee under fire home
foot prints camp side
honey noon sick after sea moon made

Use the words in the pond to make compound words.

Write a compound word that means . . .

1. tracks made by those flat things at the bottom of the legs.

   _____

2. next to the ocean

   _____

3. shining beam from the light in the night sky

   _____

4. created at the place where you live

   _____

5. buzzing insect who makes sweet sticky stuff

   _____

Tell what each compound word means.

6. afternoon _____

   _____

7. campfire _____

   _____

8. undersea _____

   _____

9. fireside _____

   _____

10. carsick _____

   _____

Name

Vocabulary: Word Meaning, Compounds
Common Core Reinforcement Activities: 2nd Grade Language

What Would You Do With It?

What would you do with a lasso? At a dude ranch in Texas, Frannie and her twin sister, Freida, are learning what to do with a lasso.

Circle the answers that tell what you would do with these other things! Use your dictionary to learn what the words mean.

What would you do with . . .

1. . . . a snowdrift?
   a. send it to a friend
   b. jump in it
   c. cook it

2. . . . an omelet?
   a. bury it
   b. spend it
   c. eat it

3. . . . a canoe?
   a. paddle it
   b. make dinner in it
   c. dance with it

4. . . . a scarecrow?
   a. scare it
   b. put it in a garden
   c. give it a bath

5. . . . a blossom?
   a. spend it
   b. put it on toast
   c. smell it

6. . . . a fishhook?
   a. put salt on it
   b. hide it
   c. put a worm on it

7. . . . a diary?
   a. put a cow in it
   b. write in it
   c. swallow it

8. . . . a dessert?
   a. ride a camel through it
   b. eat it
   c. dance to it

9. . . . a slicker?
   a. wear it
   b. put it in your hair
   c. paint with it

Name

Catch a Great Wave

Here's how to catch a great wave.

Look at the word each surfer is saying.

Then write three synonyms for that word in the "speech balloons."

Synonyms are words that mean the same thing!

Vocabulary: Word Relationships
Common Core Reinforcement Activities: 2nd Grade Language

A Stop at the Pastry Shop

Frannie and friends enjoy pastries at a sidewalk table in Paris, France.
Answer these questions from today's menu.

Menu

euros

chocolate éclair — 3

caramel cream — 5

strawberry crêpe — 5

cheese pastry — 2

whipped cream cake — 7

French bread — 3

cinnamon bun — 3

apple tart — 4

lemon custard — 2

mocha shake — 4

1. The eighth item on the menu is an apple tart. Have you ever tasted anything that is **tart**? How does it taste?

   _____

2. What word on the menu names the French money?

   _____

3. The last item on the menu is a mocha crepe. What does **mocha** taste like?

   _____

   What is a **crêpe**?

   _____

   _____

4. Which pastry on the menu is the most **expensive**?

   _____

5. Which item might be the **fluffiest**?

   _____

6. Which item might be very **creamy**?

   _____

7. Which items might taste **fruity**?

   _____

Name

Word Relatives

Wilbur is off to visit his relatives at the beach. He is taking **some** stuff along. Or you could say he is taking **loads** of stuff along.

The words **some** and **loads** are like relatives. Their meanings are similar. But one has a milder meaning, and the other has a stronger meaning.

Look at each pair of words. Write each word in the correct column.

If there is only one word, write it in the correct column. Then **you** think of a word for the other column.

WORD RELATIVES		MILD MEANING	STRONG MEANING
1. like	adore	_____	_____
2. freezing	cool	_____	_____
3. genius	smart	_____	_____
4. warm		_____	_____
5. exhausted	tired	_____	_____
6. gigantic		_____	_____
7. thrilled	pleased	_____	_____
8. wicked	naughty	_____	_____
9. complain	scream	_____	_____
10. furious	angry	_____	_____

Name _____

Vocabulary: Shades of Meaning
Common Core Reinforcement Activities: 2nd Grade Language

Carnival Words

At the carnival, there are lots of things to describe. There are things to see, feel, taste, smell, and hear.

Look at each carnival picture on this page and the next page (125).

Write a sentence to describe each picture.

Use some of the words in the box.

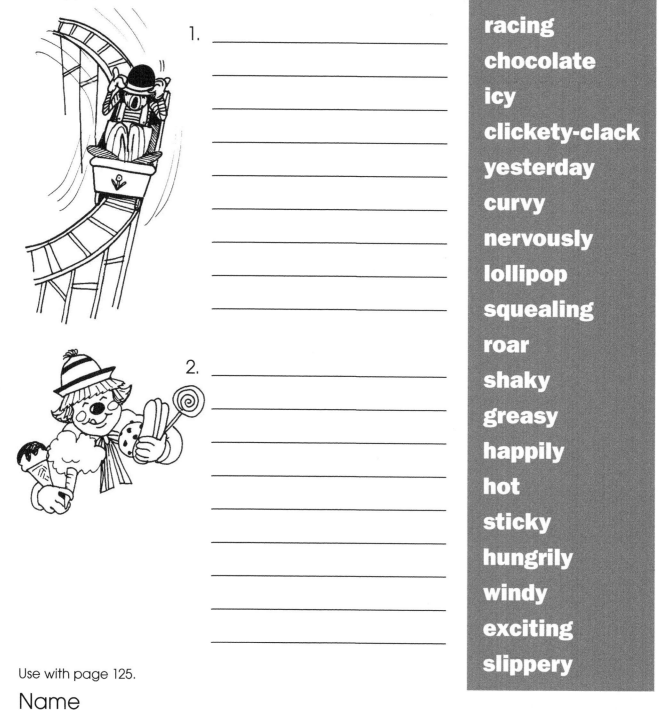

1. _____
   _____
   _____
   _____
   _____
   _____
   _____

2. _____
   _____
   _____
   _____
   _____
   _____
   _____
   _____

sweet
racing
chocolate
icy
clickety-clack
yesterday
curvy
nervously
lollipop
squealing
roar
shaky
greasy
happily
hot
sticky
hungrily
windy
exciting
slippery

Use with page 125.

Name

Carnival Words, continued

At the carnival, there are lots of things to describe. There are things to see, feel, taste, smell, and hear.

crash
screech
loud
accidentally
sleepy
slippery
icy
sleepily
later
gigantic
clumsy
longer
never
upside-down
stretch
bumpy
snoring
lazy
grumpily
scraping
suddenly
softly

3. _____
_____
_____
_____
_____

4. _____
_____
_____
_____
_____

Use with page 124.

Name

Copyright © 2014 World Book, Inc./
Incentive Publications, Chicago, IL

Acquired Vocabulary
Common Core Reinforcement Activities: 2nd Grade Language

Look Again!

Mr. Moose is seeing double today.
Each sentence he reads seems
to have two meanings!

Read each sentence. Then circle
the letter that shows the real meaning.

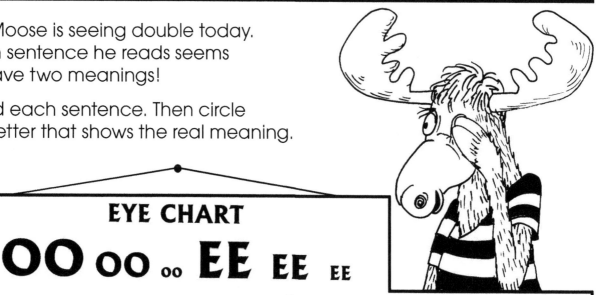

EYE CHART
OO oo oo EE EE EE

1. *Keep your eyes on that moose.*
   a. Take your eyes and put them on that moose.
   b. Keep watching that moose.

2. *I'll be right there, so hold your horses.*
   a. I'll be there soon; so be patient.
   b. I'll be there soon, so grab onto the reins of those horses and hold them.

3. *She escaped from that dog by the skin of her teeth.*
   a. She got away from the dog by using the skin on her teeth.
   b. She barely got away from that dog.

4. *My new bike cost an arm and a leg.*
   a. I had to give one arm and one leg to buy my bike.
   b. My bike cost a lot.

5. *My brother is a night owl.*
   a. My brother stays up late at night.
   b. I have a brother who is an animal—a night owl.

6. *This broken finger is really bugging me.*
   a. My finger is broken and it bothers me.
   b. My broken finger is covered with bugs.

7. *Olive went bananas when I ate her cupcake.*
   a. Olive turned into bananas when I ate her cupcake.
   b. Olive got really angry when I ate her cupcake.

8. *Joe, could you lend me your ear?*
   a. Joe, could I borrow one of your ears?
   b. Joe, could you listen to me for a while?

9. In your own words, tell what this means: *That math homework was a piece of cake!* _____

_____

Name _____

ASSESSMENT AND ANSWER KEYS

Language Arts & Literacy Assessment..**128**

    Part One: Reading...128

    Part Two: Writing...133

    Part Three: Language A—Conventions 135

    Part Four: Language B—Vocabulary 137

Assessment Answer Key **139**

Activities Answer Key **140**

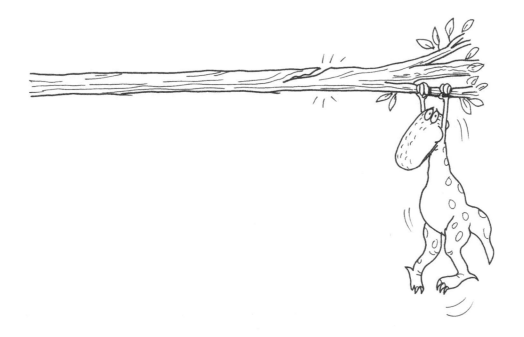

Language Arts & Literacy Assessment

PART ONE: READING

Read the poems. Circle or write an answer for each question.

A. The chubby *Plateosaurus*
Ate leaves and plants for lunch.
Its teeth wouldn't grind the chewy stuff.
So it ate rocks to add some crunch.
These stones went in its belly.
(It might sound kind of crude.)
But bellystones were helpful
To grind and smash the food.

B. *Phytosaurs* had toothy smiles.
They looked a lot like crocodiles.
They swam in water and
walked on land,
And laid their eggs along
the sand.

C. *Carnosaurus* had a lizard look.
It ran with speedy feet.
It's good its teeth were razor sharp,
Because it ate tough meat.

1. The main idea of poem **A** is
   a. The dinosaur had bad teeth.
   b. The *Plateosaurus* ate plants.
   c. The dinosaur ate rocks to help digest its food.

2. Where did *Phytosaurs* live?
   a. on land
   b. on land and in water
   c in water

3. Why did *Carnosaurus* need sharp teeth?
   a. because he was a lizard
   b. to help him eat tough meat
   c. to catch his dinner

4. What word in poem **A** means "to chop up"?
   _____

5. What does it mean that the *Phytosaurs* had "toothy smiles"?
   _____

6. What words give the idea that a dinosaur has a long body and long nose?
   _____

7. Can you tell what *Phytosaurs* eat?
   _____
   _____

Name _____

Read the story and answer the questions.

Axel, Bix, Charlie, and Dixie worked at a museum.

Their job was to put dinosaur bones together.

Axel held the tail bones in place.

Bix held the leg bones in place.

Charlie climbed the ladder to put the last bone on the head.

He was not sure this job was going to be safe.

Dixie tried to hold the ladder steady.

Charlie started to drill the hole for the wire.

Dixie sneezed and made the ladder wobble.

When the ladder wobbled, Charlie fell.

Charlie knocked Bix down.

Bix knocked Axel down.

Everyone was on the floor!

8. Why did the author write this? (Circle one answer.)
   a. to teach about museums
   b. to make you laugh
   c. to convince you to go to a museum

9. What is the meaning of the word "wobble"? (Circle one answer.)
   a. fall over
   b. break
   c. wiggle

10. Do you think Charlie is sure about his job or worried about it? _____
    Circle the part of the story that helped you decide.

11. How did the story end?

    _____

    _____

    _____

    _____

Name

Read the text. Look at the picture. Answer the questions.

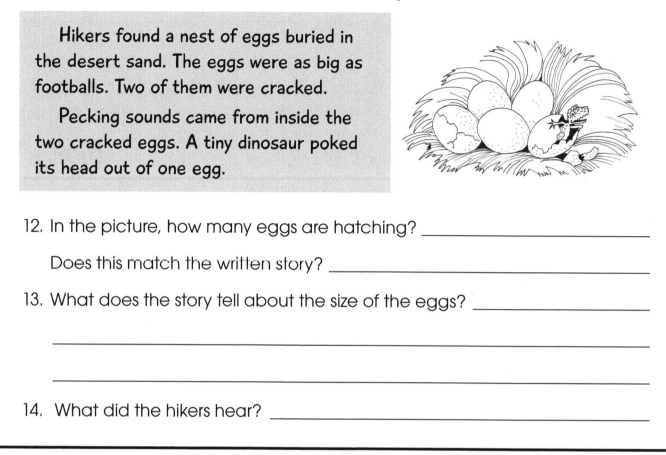

Hikers found a nest of eggs buried in the desert sand. The eggs were as big as footballs. Two of them were cracked.

Pecking sounds came from inside the two cracked eggs. A tiny dinosaur poked its head out of one egg.

12. In the picture, how many eggs are hatching? _____

    Does this match the written story? _____

13. What does the story tell about the size of the eggs? _____

    _____

    _____

14. What did the hikers hear? _____

Read the text. Look at the picture. Answer the questions.

Mom said, "Invite a friend to dinner."
I brought a *Brontosaurus*.
He acted rude and threw his food.
But he surely didn't bore us.
No, he surely didn't bore us.

15. Circle all the things that are true of the example above.
    a. It has rhyme.   b. It has rhythm.   c. It repeats words or lines.

    Why did the author use these circled things in the writing?

    _____

    _____

Name

Look at the picture to answer the question.

16. What can you tell from the picture? Circle one answer.
    a. The *Brontosaurus* just ate lunch.
    b. The water in the river is choppy.
    c. The river water is moving very fast.
    d. The animals are running from a tornado.

Use the Table of Contents to answer the questions.

17. Which chapter tells about the size of dinosaurs? _____

18. Which chapter tells about dinosaur teeth?_____

19. Would page 16 tell if the *Stegosaurus* was a plant eater? _____

20. Which pages would you read to find out about sea monsters? (Circle one answer.)
    a. 31–34
    b. 77–83
    c. 84–87

The Kids' Book of Dinosaurs

Table of Contents

Ch 1	Learning About Dinosaurs	5
	Buried Treasures	8
	Finding Fossils	15
	How Big Were They?	20
Ch 2	Dinosaur Behaviors	31
	Plant Eaters	35
	Meat Eaters	42
	Dinosaur Teeth	50
Ch 3	Kinds of Dinosaurs	60
	Swimmers	63
	Hunters	65
	Fighters	72
	Dinosaurs that Fly	77
	Sea Monsters	84
Ch 4	What Happened to the Dinosaurs?	88
Index		100

Name

Assessment
Common Core Reinforcement Activities: 2nd Grade Language

21. Circle words with **long e** or **long i** sounds.

Rap got ready to leap across the stream.

He took a giant jump to the first rock.

He hopped to the second rock.

It was slippery.

He slid across five more rocks to the other bank.

22. Circle words that have the same vowel sound as the **a** in **cake**.

maid   stayed   bead   name

23. Circle words that have the same vowel sound as **ow** in **cow**.

loud   sew   crown   flour   too

24. Circle words that have the same sound as **oi** in **boil**.

toys   bowl   coin   know   toad

25. Circle words that have the same sound as **ou** in **bought**.

caught   round   awful   toe

26. Which word means "to see again"?

review   preview   vision

27. Which word means "not able to forget"?

forgotten   unforgettable   forgot

28. Which word means "full of joy"?

rejoice   enjoyable   joyful

29. Which word means "two wheels"?

unicycle   bicycle   tricycle

30. Fix the incorrect words.

FUZZY'S CAFE

Hamburglers

Suger Cookys

Bannanna Cakes

Warm Bread

Ornge Joose

Cheeze & Crackers

Ice Creem

Name

1. Write a story about one of the pictures on this page.

   The event in the picture can happen at the beginning, in the middle, or at the end of the story.

   Make sure your story has a beginning, middle, and ending.

   _____

   _____

   _____

   _____

   _____

   _____

   _____

   _____

   _____

   _____

   _____

Name

Assessment
Common Core Reinforcement Activities: 2nd Grade Language

2. Write a paragraph to convince this dinosaur to swing on a vine. Or try to convince her NOT to swing on the vine.

Write a beginning, middle, and ending.

_____

_____

_____

_____

_____

_____

_____

_____

3. Write a paragraph explaining to this dinosaur how to fix a good lunch.

Write a beginning, clear steps, and an ending.

_____

_____

_____

_____

_____

_____

_____

Name _____

Answer the questions with words from the poster.

COME TO SEE A GREAT SHOW!
See a dinosaur baby hatch from an egg.
Ride a dinosaur yourself!
Bring a child for free!
Bring the gang for lunch!
Bring your whole team for $10!

1. Which word tells what kind of baby?

   _____

2. What word in line 3 is a pronoun?

   _____

3. What nouns include more than one person? _____ and _____

4. Circle any word on the poster that is used as a noun.

Write the plural form of the noun.	Write the past form of the verb.
5. mouse _____	10. eat _____
6. wish _____	11. bring _____
7. calf _____	12. try _____
8. child _____	13. worry _____
9. city _____	14. sing _____

Finish each sentence. Make it a complete sentence.

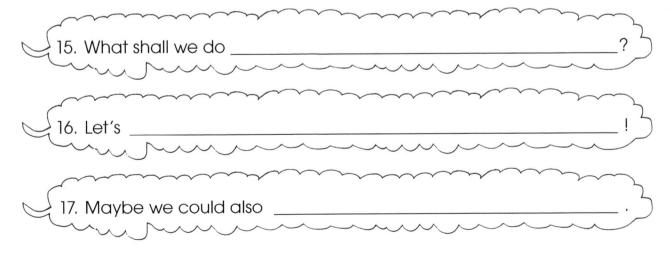

15. What shall we do _____ ?

16. Let's _____ !

17. Maybe we could also _____ .

Name _____

18. Write the commas that are missing from the letter.

19. Circle the letters in the letter that should be capitals.

july 6 2000

dear stella

Please come along with me on a bike trip on friday.

meet me by the Yammy river bridge at noon.

Lexy will join us later to play tag. she is visiting

me from the Sunshine desert.

I will see you next week.

Your friend

Pix

Stella
Stegosaurus
12

Write the contraction that can be formed from each pair of two words.

20. I am _____

21. can not _____

22. she will _____

Write the missing apostrophes.

23. The clowns hat is red.

24. The volcanos rumble was loud.

25. Lets catch the dinosaurs tail!

Find the words that are spelled wrong. Write each one correctly.

peple   freind   please   talk

magic   dissappear   dentist

dollar   wolves   baloon   tryed

26. _____

27. _____

28. _____

29. _____

30. _____

Name _____

Read the story and answer the questions.

Two young dinosaurs chased each other and romped happily. The playful friends chased each other in circles. Then they ran like lightning across the desert. After an hour, they were exhausted. They fell asleep, as quick as a wink.

1. What does **romped** mean?
   a. fought
   b. played
   c. slept

2. Which word in the story means "full of play"?

   _____

3. Which word in the story means "very tired"?

   _____

4. The friends "ran like lightning."

   What does this mean?
      a. They got caught in a thunderstorm.
      b. The friends were hit by lightning.
      c. The friends ran very fast.

5. They fell asleep "as quick as a wink."

   What does this mean?

   They fell asleep _____

   _____

rewrite
agreeable
midtown
disagree
writer
friendless
under
slide
friendship
water

Write a word from the dinosaur's list to match each meaning.

6. without friends_____

7. opposite of agree _____

8. in the middle of town _____

9. write again _____

Create a compound word from two of the words on the list.

10. _____

Name

**Circle one answer
for each question.**

11. Where would you find
    a **sandwich**?

    a. on a hat

    b. in a shoe

    c. in a lunchbox

12. Where would you find
    an **engine**?

    a. in a throat

    b. on a train

    c. in a grocery bag

13. Which of these would you find
    in a **refrigerator**?

    a. a nostril

    b. a stethoscope

    c. an avocado

14. Which of these words is a
    stronger way to say **talk**?

    say   speak   insist

15. Which of these words is the
    strongest way to say the idea?

    cool   cold   freezing

**Circle the best word
for each sentence.**

16. If you pinch me, I will _____
    very loud!

    a. sing

    b. squeal

    c. whisper

    d. moan

17. Stella was afraid to climb the tree
    because it looked too _____.

    a. short

    b. tall

    c. flimsy

    d. strong

18. What a good day to be out in the
    _____!

    a. desert

    b. dessert

    c. deserve

19. Yesterday, we had the _____
    thunderstorm.

    a. wrist

    b. worst

    c. worth

20. These are all different meanings
    of the same word. Decide what
    the word is. Write it on the line.

    a. not heavy

    b. something that shines

    c. to start a fire

    The word is _____

Name _____

Assessment Answer Key

Part One: Reading

1. c
2. b
3. b
4. grind
5. teeth hung out of their mouths; or they had big teeth
6. "They looked a lot like crocodiles."
7. No, the poem does not tell what they eat.
8. b
9. c
10. worried; Circle: He was not sure this job was going to be safe.
11. Everyone fell. Everyone was on the floor.
12. two; yes
13. They were as big as footballs.
14. pecking sounds
15. a, b, c; Answers to the second part will vary. They made the story/poem more interesting and fun to read.
16. b, c
17. Ch 1
18. Ch 2
19. no
20. c
21. Circle: ready, leap, stream, He, giant, slippery, five
22. maid, stayed, name
23. loud, crown, flour
24. toys, coin
25. caught, awful
26. review
27. unforgettable
28. joyful
29. bicycle
30. Hamburgers, Sugar, Cookies, Banana, Orange, Juice, Cheese, Cream

Part Two: Writing

1. Check to see that story has a beginning, a middle that tells some detail about the event, and an ending. The story should have some connection to one of the pictures.
2. Check to see that paragraph has a beginning, a position (opinion or argument) with at least one reason, and some conclusion.
3. Check to see that paragraph has a beginning, a few clear explanatory steps in sensible sequence, and an ending.

Part Three: Language A—Conventions

1. dinosaur
2. yourself
3. gang and team
4. Circle: show, baby, egg, dinosaur, child, gang, lunch, team
5. mice
6. wishes
7. calves
8. children
9. cities
10. ate
11. brought
12. tried
13. worried
14. sang
15.–17. Sentences will vary. Check to see that they are complete, sensible sentences.
18. Insert commas after: 6, stella, friend
19. Circle first letter of: july, dear, stella, friday, meet, river, bridge, she, desert
20. I'm
21. can't
22. she'll
23. clown's
24. volcano's
25. Let's; dinosaur's
Answers for 26–30 can be in any order.
26. people
27. friend
28. disappear
29. balloon
30. tried

Part Four: Language B—Vocabulary

1. b
2. playful
3. exhausted
4. c
5. fast
6. friendless
7. disagree
8. midtown
9. rewrite
10. Answers will vary. (waterslide, underwater, underwriter)
11. c
12. b
13. c
14. insist
15. freezing
16. b
17. c
18. a
19. b
20. light

Activities Answer Key

Note: There are many cases in which answers may vary. Accept an answer if student can give a reasonable justification or details to support it, or if you can see the sense in it.

Reading-Literature (pages 22–40)

page 22
1. c
2. Drawings will vary.
3. a roaring noise; a big furry shape; two big red eyes

page 23
Check drawings to see that the listed items have been included and properly placed.
Main idea: At this school, students learn in the outdoors.

page 24
Check drawings to see that 1–6 directions are followed and that the final instruction on the page has been followed.
There are 2 crabs.

page 25
A. 3, 4, 6
B. Randall Rat
C. Flossie Frog
D. He is a beaver. He is brown. He bounced balls.

page 26
1. Find a way to monitor the students' retelling of the story.
2. b

page 27
1. Find a way to monitor the students' retelling of stories.
2. Answers will vary: The elephant's nose became long because a crocodile grabbed his nose and stretched it.

page 28
Answers may vary somewhat. These show the general idea.
1. They were good sports. They congratulated the other team.
2. The coach told the team they played well.
3. They were sad but they gave a cheer for the winning team.

page 29
1. c
2. He went home and made a bigger list that he could keep in front of his eyes.

page 30
1. talk and chalk; mind and kind
2. 1 and 7
3. Answers may vary; to show how important the rule is
4. #5; the "m" sound
5. Answers will vary.

page 31
1. red: sounds; *toot, toot, toot; twang, twang, twang; tune; ding, ping, clang*
2. blue: sights; *slurpy paints; drip, drip, drip; draw; design; stripes; squiggly lines*
3. Answers will vary.

page 32
Answers will vary.
1. Pedro wanted to play a good game, so he practiced a lot.
2. Pedro hit the ball and broke a window.
3. Pedro got a home run.

page 33
1. We are studying addition and subtraction.
2. The problems are on page 21.
3. There are 22 problems in all.
4. The assignment is due tomorrow.
5. Let's study together.

page 34
Answers will vary.
A. Thoughts show that Flossie is very happy watching clouds.
B. Thoughts show that Flossie feels she should be doing her homework.

page 35
1. Four
2. apples
3. fish
4. butterfly
5. ball
6. lemonade
7. Answers will vary.

page 36
Names of characters are, from left to right:
thief, prince, queen, queen's maid, princess
1 and 2—Answers will vary. Check to see that answers have enough information to show that the student has examined the picture and has reasons for the answer.

page 37
1. Suki Skunk – line to lower right skunk
2. Flossie Frog – line straight up to opera singer
3. Benjy Beaver—line to harp-player below box
4. Pedro Porcupine – line to porcupine on left
5. Suzie Squirrel – line to ballet dancer in lower left corner
6. Becky Bunny – line straight right to gymnast
7. Ricki Raccoon—line to upper left corner to raccoon

page 38
1. Benjy
2. Becky
3. Sammy
4. Suzie
5. Flossie
6. Pedro
7. Ricki

pages 39–40
Answers will vary.
1. Students might say that stories have same topics; they are about the same characters; they go along with the same pictures; and they give the same idea.
2. Students might say the style on page 39 has paragraphs and page 40 has stories in poem form. They might mention the rhyme. They might say the poems are fun.

page 42
1. sandwiches
2. 26
3. pizza
4. 8
5. 9
6. 20
7. pizzas
8. 10

page 43
1. lizard
2. thick
3. pink and yellow
4. slowly
5. North America

page 44
Answers may vary.
1. The dragon
2. An animal ate the cookies.
3. The scorpions got loose and scared somebody.
4. The raccoon will get into the garbage can.

page 45
1. cherry
2. pickle
3. tomato
4. corn
5. worm

page 46
1. c
2. a
3. b

page 47
1. roots
2. stem
3. leaves
4. flower
5. cone
Check drawings for accuracy. See that all named plant parts are shown in drawings.

page 48
1. c
2. b
3. c
4. b
5. b
6. a

page 49
1. Library
2. Fire Department
3. Police
4. Parks Office
5. Water Services
6. Ambulance or police
7. Post Office
8. Garbage Collection
9. Animal Control
10. Power Company

page 50
1. C
2. C
3. A
4. D
5. D
6. H
7. D
8. M

page 51
Pictures and captions will vary.

page 52
1. B
2. F
3. E
4. G
5. D
6. C
7. A
8. Answers will vary. The most likely purpose is that the author wanted to teach about the parts of a flower.

page 53
Goods path includes these words: gardener, baker, automaker, builder, cook, artist, farmer, shoemaker, tent maker

Services path includes these words: firefighter, janitor, auto salesperson, piano teacher, banker, waiter, doctor, baseball player, plumber, librarian, grocery store clerk, animal trainer, president, mayor, police officer

Answer to final question about author's purpose will vary. The most likely purpose is that the author wanted to explain about goods and services and give examples.

page 54
1. yes
2. one
3. no
4. three
5. no
6. yes

page 55
Answers will vary. Listen to explanations for answers. See that students give valid reasons for their answers. Look for connections between their answers and what they "read" in the illustrations.

page 56
Top row: red, green box, green
Center row: brown, (milk truck), brown
Bottom row: red, yellow, orange

page 57
Answers may vary.
1. The river was so wild that the raft tipped over and dumped the dogs into the water.
2. They probably had to swim a long way to shore.

page 58
Parts students choose to circle for substantiation of answers may vary.
1. yes (Circle the first, second, third, seventh, and last lines in red.)
2. yes (Circle 7th line in blue.)
3. yes (Circle 5th line in green.)
4. science, art (Circle 7th and 8th lines in purple.)

page 59
Answers may vary.
The texts on both pages give information about specific dinosaurs.

page 60
Answers may vary.
The texts on page 59 are in paragraphs. The texts on page 61 are poems. They give information in a different way. The poems have rhyme, while the paragraphs do not.

Reading-Foundational Skills (pages 62–78)

page 62
Connect an—big—cop—did—egg—fox—gum—hot—it—jet—kit—lid—mop—nod—on—pot—quack—red—sun—top—up—van—win—X ray—yes—zip

page 63
Check to see that the drawings reflect accurately followed directions.
The following long-vowel words should be circled.
1. bow, hair
2. smile, face
3. kite, air
4. kite
5. ice, cream, cone
6. nose
7. cape, green
8. rose, shoe
9. cupcake
10. balloon

page 64
Words can be listed in any order.
goofy
moose
loose
deep
woods
Look
see
feet
foot
needs
cool
pools
looking
food
feed

toadstools
beetles
too
zoo
free
There are 20 words.

page 65
Circle: beast, be, related, early, These, many, seek, egrets, egrets, feet, egrets, quickly, eat, meal

page 66
Color the clouds with the following words and join them with a path: tow, low, know, mow, show, grow, snow, flow

page 67
1. boat
2. loud
3. beach
4. rain

page 68
Paths will vary. Have student read words to demonstrate that each path follows instructions. The shortest path will vary depending on the route the student chose.

page 69
1. retired
2. sleepy
3. friendly or friendless
4. beautiful
5. restless or restful
6. unhappy
7. disappointed

page 70
1. size
2. appear
3. poison
4. Quiet

5. strange
6. peace
7. large
8. power

page 71
1. stop
2. danger
3. work
4. agree
5. blame
6. fine
7. neighbor
8. care
9. tame
10. friend

page 72
Down
1. reigned
3. sales
4. blew
5. plane
9. here
10. dew
Across
2. pairs
5. pare
6. tale
7. way
8. sea
10. dear
11. knew

page 73
Monitor the reading of these words to check for word recognition.

page 74
1. thought
2. early
3. Why
4. build
5. different
6. eyes
7. toward

8. again

page 75
Line should connect words in this order: afraid, another, beautiful, blue, buried, caught, different, dolphin, heard, light, mystery, octopus, oyster, please, ready, sneaky, surprise, walk, where, wriggle

The creature is a hermit crab.

page 76
The path follows these words: because, right, which, ramp, people, scares, through, there, write, when, quiet, friend, scream, where, animal, thought, worst, leaves, thumb, though, believe
Bottom puzzle: mosquitoes

page 77
1. rain
2. jungle
3. parrot
4. banana
5. monkey
6. jaguar
7. raft
8. leaf
9. vine
10. river
11. anaconda

page 78
Monitor student reading/recognition and definitions of words.

Writing (pages 80–94)

pages 80-81
Check to see that written paragraph has a beginning, clearly stated opinion and at least one clear supporting reason, and a clear ending.

page 82
Check to see that written paragraph (or paragraphs) has a beginning, clearly stated opinion and at least one clear supporting reason, and a clear ending.

page 83
Check to see that written paragraph (or paragraphs) has a beginning, clearly stated opinion and at least one clear supporting reason, and a clear ending.

page 84
Check to see that the writing includes clear information, a beginning, and an end.

page 85
Check to see that writing includes clear instructions in logical sequence, and that there is a satisfying ending.

page 86
Check to see that writing includes sensible rules (though they can be frivolous) in complete sentences.

page 87
Check to see that story has a clear beginning, events, and ending.

page 88
Check to see that the writing for each diver contains a clear idea expressed in a complete sentence or sentences.

page 89
Check for logical questions, some with connections to the picture, written in complete sentence form. Assist students in reviewing and revising their writing.

page 90
Check for a sensible invitation that includes information needed for the event. Check to see that sentences are complete. Assist students in reviewing and revising their writing.

page 91
Check for sensible conclusions to the poems, written in complete sentence form. Assist students in reviewing and revising their writing.

page 92
Check for complete, sensible sentences to finish the comparisons. Assist students in reviewing and revising their writing.

page 93
Work with students as they research the topic. Oversee the production and sharing of their "Five Things I Learned...".

page 94
Work with students as they recall their own knowledge and experience or research the topic. Oversee the production and sharing of their completed sentences.

Language (pages 96–126)

page 96
1. bundle
2. umbrella
3. school
4. herd
5. yaks
6. kitchen
7. iguana
8. troop
9. tongue
10. eggs
11. nose
Bushy kitten

page 97
First row:
mice, bunnies, bears, knives
Second row:
cameras, butterflies, puppies, turtles
Third row:
fish, glasses, radios, monkeys
Fourth row:
ducks, pennants, hippos

pages 98-99
First answer shows what verb should be circled in the clue. Second answer shows past tense verb for the puzzle.
DOWN
1. bring; brought
2. enjoy; enjoyed
8. raises; raised
9. dry; dried
13. cries; cried
15. meet; met
ACROSS
3. hear; heard
4. go; went
5. find; found
6. lose; lost
7. hurry; hurried
10. bites; bit
11. draw; drew
12. rise; rose
14. worries; worried
16. become; became

page 100
Color cups & saucers 1, 2, 4, 6

page 101
1. adjectives circled in green: lucky, purple, big
   30 points
2. adjectives circled in green: six, good; adverb circled in red: loudly
   25 points
3. adjectives circled in green: new, striped, important
   30 points
4. adjectives circled in green: first, straight; adverbs circled in red: smoothly, down
   30 points
5. adjectives circled in green: four, noisy, teenage
   30 points
6. adjectives circled in green: second, highest; adverb circled in red: easily
   25 points
7. adjectives circled in green: pink, cotton; adverbs circled in red: suddenly
   25 points
8. adjectives circled in green: long, winning
   20 points
Final question: answer is yes.
Total points: 215

page 102
1. slowly
2. soon
3. down
4. Carefully
5. ahead
6. tightly
7. never
8. frequently
9. deeply
10. Soon
11. Suddenly
12. rapidly
13. safely
14. Tomorrow

page 103
1-8: Sentences will vary. Check to see that student has written complete sentences.

page 104
1-10: Sentences will vary. Check to see that student has written complete sentences.
Likely colors:
Blue: 1, 6, 9
Red: 2, 4, 8, 10
Yellow: 3, 5, 7

page 105
Answers may vary some. Accept any reasonable questions.
1. Is that Ellie on the high wire?
2. Is it true that the elephant can fly?
3. Can Ellie juggle pies?
4. Does Ellie know how to ride a unicycle?
5. Was the elephant jumping through a ring of fire?
6. Has Ellie eaten all the cotton candy?

page 106
1. 40¢; the, long, beach, california
2. 20¢; zelda, chester
3. 30¢; have, screaming, eagle
4. 30¢; we, valentine's day
5. 40¢; the, central, city, february

Activities Answer Key

6. 30¢; the, united, states
7. 40¢; did, monday, tuesday, wednesday
8. 40¢; lolly, molly, cannonball, Saturday
9. 40¢; did, polly, cannonball, july
10. 10¢; someone

Total: $3.20

page 107
Left-hand letter:
Insert commas after Clowntown, 10 (in date), Bella, and friend.
Right-hand letter:
Insert commas after Clowntown, 11, Bella, and friend

page 108
1. can't
2. Don't
3. horse's
4. giraffe's
5. Shouldn't
6. won't
7. elephant's
8. merry-go-round's

page 109
1. poodle
2. dishes
3. dripped
4. cough
5. valleys
6. tomorrow
7. glasses
8. would
9. pianos
10. thumb
11. babies
12. elves

page 110
Path should connect these words in any order and the words should be rewritten correctly.
thay—they
meny—many
sed—said
duz—does
gon—gone
ar—are
laff—laugh
brot—brought
beautaful—beautiful
pepel—people

suprize—surprise
anser—answer
wher—where
dubble—double
choise—choice
wether—whether or weather
wunce—once

page 111
Assist students as they find words in dictionaries or other sources.
1. descend
2. engineer
3. twelve
4. clapped
5. everybody
6. yesterday

page 112
Color pins:
1, 2, 3, 6, 8, 9
Total score is 29

page 113
Answers will vary. Accept reasonable answers, showing students have used context to determine meanings.
1. report about what weather is going to be
2. pushed
3. loud screaming sound
4. bumpy
5. many times; often
6. gone

page 114
1. a
2. b
3. b
The likely thief is Peter.

page 115
Answers will vary. Accept reasonable answers, showing students have used context to determine meanings.
1. Be polite.
2. refuse
3. loud screaming
4. drop
5. slope
6. Skiers who act wild will not be allowed.

page 116
1. danger
2. appeared
3. not possible
4. move again or move away
5. not protected
6. together

page 117
1. wave
2. sink
3. run
4. star
5. jam
6. drop

page 118
Left column roots:
like, fear, fruit, cycle, sphere, kind, fear
1. fruity
2. hemisphere
3. dislike
4. kindly
5. fearful
Right column roots:
slow, cycle, bake, build, bake, sense
6. baker
7. build again
8. nonsense
9. slowly
10. one wheel

page 119
1. footprints
2. seaside
3. moonlight
4. homemade
5. honeybee
Answers below will vary.
6. later than 12 p.m.
7. burning wood near the place where you sleep outside
8. beneath the ocean
9. next to something burning
10. not feeling well riding in a vehicle

page 120
1. b
2. c
3. a
4. b
5. c
6. c
7. b
8. b
9. a

page 121
Answers will vary. Check to see that choices of words work as synonyms for the three words and apply well to the context.

page 122
1. Answers will vary. (bitter, sting your tongue, etc)
2. euros
3. Mocha tastes like coffee or coffee and chocolate. A crêpe is a rolled-up, thin pancake.
4. whipped cream cake
5. Answers will vary.
6. Answers will vary.
7. Answers will vary. (strawberry crêpe, apple tart, lemon custard)

page 123
1. like; adore
2. cool; freezing
3. smart; genius
4. warm; answers will vary (hot, scalding, blistering)
5. tired; exhausted
6. answers will vary (large, big); gigantic
7. pleased; thrilled
8. naughty; wicked
9. complain; scream
10. angry; furious

pages 124–125
Written sentences will vary. Check to see that student has used some of the suggested words in complete, descriptive sentences.

page 126
1. b
2. a
3. b
4. b
5. a
6. a
7. b
8. b
9. Answers may vary: That math homework was easy.